HA-HA! HORROR

COLLECTOR'S EDITION
BY
MONSTERMATT PATTERSON

Mystery and Horror, LLC
Clearwater, Florida

HA-HA! HORROR COLLECTOR'S EDITION

Copyright © 2020 by Mystery and Horror, LLC
Collector's Edition

Printed with the permission of the author.
All rights reserved.

No portion of this publication may be reproduced, stored in any electronic system, copied or transmitted in any form or by any means, electronic, digital, mechanical, photocopy, recording or otherwise without the written permission of the author. This includes any storage of the author's work on any information storage and retrieval system.
This is a work of fiction. Any resemblance to any actual person living or dead, or to any known location is the coincidental invention of the author's creative mind.

Printed in USA by Mystery and Horror, LLC
ISBN-13: 978-1-949281-11-8

(Mystery and Horror, LLC)
(www.mysteryandhorrorllc.com)

BOOK PRAISE AND PREJUDICE

"I laughed, I groaned, I shook my head in disbelief....Ha-Ha! Horror will bring a grin to the faces of adults and kids alike..."
        Colleen Wanglund Monster
        Librarian

"Monstermatt's Bad Monster Jokes are more fun than Zombies at a brain buffet!"
        Dr. Gangrene
        Award winning Horror host

"Assly is the king of the Crappy Puppets and knows Craptastic Awesomeness when he sees it and that is exactly what Ha-Ha! Horror is."
        Assly the Puppet/Assly TV

"If you thought MonsterMatt's Bad Monster Jokes broke your funny bone, then Ha-Ha! Horror is going to nuke it."
        Tony Faville
        Author: *Kings of the Dead* and *Avery Nolan: Private Dick of the Dead*

"Once Upon A Time... Monsters were all nice... then they heard some of Monstermatt's jokes."
        Author Mike Aloisi

"Monstermatt's jokes could raise a laugh from the dead... in fact they've been known to raise the dead..."
        Maria Olsen
        Paranormal Activity 3

"Monstermatt's Bad Jokes inspired my own:
Q: What do you get when you cross a werewolf with a redneck?
A: Nothing. Some things a werewolf just ain't gonna do."
        Bill Oberst Jr.
        Abraham Lincoln vs. Zombies

WELCOME TO HA-HA! HORROR

In Loving Memory of my mother Jean and my grandmother Mary

This is dedicated to my wife Deanna and our children: Sarah, Grant and Emma.

TABLE OF CONTENTS

Introduction	i
Igor and the Master	iii
Chapter 1 Basket Case	1
Chapter 2 The Island of Dr Moreau	3
Chapter 3 The Blob	5
Chapter 4 Killer Klowns from Outer Space	7
Chapter 5 Christine	9
Chapter 6 Universal Monsters	11
Chapter 7 Street Trash	13
Chapter 8 Kaiju! God(zilla) Bless You!	15
Chapter 9 Trog	17
Chapter 10 Faces of Death	19
Chapter 11 Return of the Living Dead	51
Chapter 12 Motel Hell	53
Chapter 13 Miscellaneous Horror	55
Chapter 14 Miscellaneous Jokes	69
Chapter 15 My Soul to Take 3D	107
Chapter 16 Black Swan	109

Chapter 17 Insidious — 111

Chapter 18 The Last Exorcism — 113

Chapter 19 Vampire Girl vs. Frankenstein Girl — 115

Chapter 20 My Bloody Valentine — 117

Chapter 21 Rubber — 119

Chapter 22 Splice — 121

Chapter 23 Piranha 3D — 123

Chapter 24 Superheroes and Cartoons — 125

Chapter 25 Aliens — 155

Chapter 26 The Manitou — 157

Chapter 27 Slime City — 159

Chapter 28 Daybreakers — 161

Chapter 29 Troll Hunter — 163

Chapter 30 Dead Snow — 165

Chapter 31 Ho! Ho! Horror — 167

Chapter 32 Prometheus — 169

Chapter 33 Western Horror Films — 171

Chapter 34 Final Destination Films — 173

Chapter 35 Children of the Corn — 187

Chapter 36 Don't be Afraid of the Dark — 189

Chapter 37 The Monstermatt Minute — 191

Chapter 38 Ho Ho Horrordays	193
Chapter 39 Chriptmas Scare-ols	195
Chapter 40 Rancid Rhymes	201
Afterward	i
Acknowledgements	iv
About the Author	ix

INTRODUCTION BY MICHAEL BONE DIGGER

Matt has been abusing our site now for quite some time with his awful creations. In fact it's fair to say that it's a clear sign that the world is coming to an end when publishers agree to unleash these stinkers upon the masses.

Matt's humor falls somewhere between 70's Dixie Cups and the wrappers of old Bazooka Joe gum. There's a reason they're not trendy anymore.

I'm still in awe how anyone has this much time on their hands to write such bad humor. Even Chuck Norris had to look away...and Norris never looks away from anything.

Michael Bone Digger
HorrorNews.net

IGOR AND THE MASTER

Pssst! Igor! How's it look out there?

Master, it's a packed house- standing TOMB only! Don't blow it!

Igor, as if that were even possible! As you know, being The Man of a Thousand Bad Monster Jokes requires a certain level of talent and "je ne SEANCE quoi" that is not known to most living creatures. Hold my coffee. I got this!

#GhoulMourningManiacs!!! Mwhuhuhuahahaha!!
Yesssssshhhh! That's right. It is I, your fiend, yours DROOL-ly! Monstermatt Patterson The Man of a Thousand Bad Monster Jokes hailing all the way from Mattsylvania! Look! I see the Thing that sits in the corner of the tomb is here!

Heyyy-o! You, creepy Thing you.

Well, here's what we've been up to, since we last met. Igor has been helping me around the laboratory and not making too much of a mess.

I've been conducting valuable research, like why is Avocado toast a thing?! The only thing greener than that, is Frankenstein's Monster after Ted Turner and his colorization got a hold of him!

I've been watching tons of monster movies, sci-fi movies, reading books and magazines about them.

Yes, I can read. It's gotten to be a bit much. I think I'm in a state of SCHLOCK!!

So, if you're wondering why you're here, it's because you know that you can laugh at me or with me. It's fine. No, really. I want you to LAUGH,

GUFFAW, SNORT, CHORTLE, and GROAN, with every gag, joke and toon in this tome. As of this printing, I've written over 2700 Bad Monster Jokes and this is a healthy serving of such fare! There's a ton of material here, not as much as is required to make The Amazing Colossal Man a suit of clothes,
but a ton nonetheless!

Maniacs! Turn the page and dive in! Swoop in like The Giant Claw! I'll be your Bacon, I mean BEAK-on of laughter!

Yeah, we're gonna WING it, but I'm no TURKEY! Go on! There's nothing to lose, but that furrowed brow.

CHAPTER 1
BASKET CASE

Basket Case is a horror comedy directed by Frank Henenlotter and tells the story of two brothers, Duane and Belial. They were born Siamese Twins and Belial was a mutated freak. They were separated and sought revenge.

Who doesn't love a good family film?

Who doesn't love bad jokes that'll have you asking, "What's in the box?"

Why did Duane and Belial's surgeon separate them?
They came to a split decision!

Duane got so drunk that he almost dropped Belial, basket and all.
I guess he couldn't hold his wicker!

What is Duane and Belial's favorite Lionel Richie song?
"Stuck on You!"

What is Belial's favorite Wizard of Oz character?
The "Wicker" Witch of the West!

What does Belial eat for his midday meal?
Box Lunch!

What is Belial's favorite Devo lyric?
"Wicker! Wicker good!"

If Damien replaced Duane, Belial would have a "Thorne" in his side!

Did you hear that Duane & Belial teamed up with Bruce Springsteen?

Yeah, they're called "BOSS-ket Case!"

What do you get by crossing Duane & Belial with an upholstered sofa-shaped box?
"Basket CHAISE!"

Kind of makes you feel like LOUNGING around, right?

Did you know Belial loved a certain cut of meat?
He was a real BRISKET Case!

Duane & Belial were mechanics. Yeah, they're real GASKET Cases!

Belial was an unorthodox intellectual. You could say he thought inside the box!

Any emails from Duane & Belial come with an attachment.

The Basket Case had tickets to a concert. They had BOX seats in the B-AISLE. They had to DUANE their bank account to pay for them.

CHAPTER 2
THE ISLAND OF DR MOREAU

The Island of Dr. Moreau is a story by H.G. Wells that tells the tale of a scientist who creates "Animal-men" by scientifically combining humans and animals. Not some cheap photoshop tricks! They adopt rules: "No spill blood," "Not walk on all fours," etc. and create a society. Let's bring some kibble and chew on some "yuks!"

Did you hear Dr. Moreau gives makeovers?
He promises a "whole GNU EWE!"

Which Vancouver Canuck hails from Dr. Moreau's Island?
Dave TIGER Williams!

Who's the best comedian on the doctor's island?
John "BULLushi!!"

Which of Dr. Moreau's creations can "Turn the world on with her smile?"
Mary TIGER Moore!

Some of the island's Animal-Men were known "to COW" the others.

Oh, you didn't like that one? Hold on, VEAL be right back!

What song did Dr Doolittle sing when he arrived on Dr Moreau's island of 1/2 men and 1/2 beasts?
If I could talk to the "Manimals"!

What Go-Go's song do they like on Dr Moreau's island?
We Got The "Beast"!

What does the "International House of Pancakes" have in common with Dr Moreau's "Island House of Pain"?

Either way, "IHOP" hurts!!

What inspired Dr Moreau to start his experiments?
He overheard a feminist say: "Men are Pigs!" He thought that was a good start!

What Man/Beast on Dr Moreau's island is a famous author?
Kurt "Vonne-Goat"!

One of the laws on Dr Moreau's island says, "No Spill Blood." So, if the Crips ever show up, they'll need a truce.

One of the Manimals, a man/pig, wanted to grow a moustache. What kind?
A "Handle-Boar" Moustache!

A Jewish cousin of that Manimal was supposed to celebrate his "Boar Mitsvah"!

CHAPTER 3
THE BLOB

The Blob is a sci-fi treat about a mountainous, gelatinous creature from space that terrorizes cities, gobbling up everything in its path. Kind of like most teenagers during a growth spurt! Let's see if some jokes can outlast the jelly-filled monster, because jam don't shake like that!

What Johnny Paycheck song was inspired by The Blob?
"Take This 'Blob' and Shove It!"

Why did the nightclub hire The Blob?
To make Jell-O Shots!!

What kids' program do the jiggly, elastic-like Blob's children watch?
The Wiggles!

What alien creeps and leaps, sliding across the floor, of an ice-cream parlor with 31 flavors?
Baskin "Blob-ins"!

What kind of Blob toy are they going to make?
A Blob-ble-head!

What do you get by crossing a reggae singer and an enormous gelatinous alien?
"Blob" Marley!

What do you get by crossing a gelatinous space alien and the choreographer of *Cabaret, Chicago,* and more?
"BLOB" Fosse!

What do you say to the Blob when he's feeling envious?
"You JELLY?"

What did the Blob eat that disagreed with him?
The Debate Team!

What should you do when the lamp burns out? Change the "Light-Blob!"

The Blob's theme song states that "He creeps and leaps and glides across the floor."
Heck, I do that at most wedding receptions after cocktails!

What does the gelatinous fiend do for Halloween?
He goes "BLOBBING for apples!!"

CHAPTER 4
KILLER KLOWNS FROM OUTER SPACE

Killer Klowns From Outer Space is a cult film from the Chiodo Brothers. In it, the Klowns terrorize a small town with their space circus of terror. It's not all cotton candy and fun! Oh no, they mean some serious business. So, let's get serious right back at them and battle them with some bad jokes! I'm a clown, they are Klowns. What's a little humor between FIENDS?

What do you get for the Killer Klowns on Father's Day?
Killer Colognes from Outer Space!
Popcorn being used as a weapon!
Cotton Candy cocoons!

Is it a movie theater concession stand riot, or is it Killer Klown methods?!

What do you get by crossing a film about murderous alien Klowns and Klondike ice cream bars?
Killer "Klons" from Outer Space!

What do you get by crossing Killer Klowns with "Welcoming Back" the "Sweathogs"?
Killer Klowns from "Kotter-Space"!

What horror movie has alien Klowns that look like Seal's ex-wife?
Killer Klums From Outer Space!

Which strange life form has the worst face paint?
A) Killer Klown
B) Mimi, from The Drew Carey Show
C) Gene Simmons

A) Killer Klown wants to eat you.
B) Mimi wants to date you.

C) Gene Simmons wants to merchandise you!

What kind of commute involves The Joker, Pennywise the Clown and the Killer Klowns from Outer Space?
Car Fooling!

What film is about Klowns that overpower their victims?
Quell-er" Klowns From Outer Space !

What film is about Klowns wearing traditional Scottish garb?
"Kilt-ed" Klowns from Outer Space!

What do you get by crossing awful clowns with a cartoon gorilla?
"MAGILLA Klowns From Outer Space!"

Which clowns like ice fishing?
"Killer Klowns From AUGER Space!"

What do you get by crossing the star of "Zoolander" with nasty space clowns?
"Ben Stiller Klowns From Outer Space!"

Did you know the Killer Klowns went to Military School?
They were the Killer Klowns From ABOUT FACE!"

CHAPTER 5
CHRISTINE

Christine is a Stephen King story about a boy and his car. Wonderful! Well, except that the car is somehow possessed and possessive of the boy named Arnie. Christine the car is jealous and starts to regenerate herself into mint condition.

I think she'd be a candidate for a DIY show! Let's go BUMPER to BUMPER and get REVVED UP with some *Christine* jokes…

Arnie made so many trips to scrap yards with Christine and loaded her up that every now and then she really did have "junk in her trunk"!

Christine got rid of so many people that the mob was going to offer her a job!

Why was Christine against "Carfax" reports?
She didn't want to reveal her age or her real paint job color!

What happens when Stephen King's *Christine* gets put in jail?
She gets "InCARcerated"!

How did Christine reverse her mileage and look so good?
A decent plastic surgeon or mechanic. Either way, it's at a "body shop"!

What is one of Christine's favorite rock groups?
The "Cars"!

Who is Christine's favorite male singer?
"Axle" Rose!

Who does Christine think is a hunk?
Mr. Goodwrench!

Asked if she wanted to get *Repossessed*, Christine drove away! She didn't realize Arnie meant to go and buy that film on DVD.

Who is Christine's favorite country singer?
Freddy "Fender"!!

What do you get by crossing Stephen King's *Christine*, Neve Campbell and a meat eater?
A "CarNEVEore!"

What comedy makes Christine the car sad?
"Dude, Where's My Car?"

Did you know Christine was a successful farmer? She always has BUMPER crops!

If humans moisturize, does Christine CLEAR COAT?

Why is Christine a great Hockey player?
She "DRIVES to the net!"

CHAPTER 6
THE UNIVERSAL MONSTERS

The Phantom of the Opera. Frankenstein's Monster. Wolfman. Dracula. The Mummy. These are just some of the original wave of movie monsters, that ELECTRIFIED (sorry Franky) theatre audiences. They're the O.G. of Monsters if you will. Some more "O" than others. (I'm looking at you, Mummy!)

Then, there's The Creature from the Black Lagoon, Mole People and others that followed years later and kept the BLOOD pumping. (Whoops, sorry, Drac!) They brought in lots of SCRATCH (sorry, Wolfman) for movie studios.

Anyway, I'm dying to poke fun at these Monsters!

After getting brought to life by an enormous amount of electricity, you could say Frankenstein was up on "current" events.

What did Frankenstein want to do after receiving all that electricity?
"Spark" up some conversation!

Why was Frankenstein unsure whether to go to the doctor or tailor?
He wanted to complain about a "stitch" in his side!

What's the one way you can compare Frankenstein's stitches with bed sheets?
The Thread Count!!

Jersey Shore has "The Situation". What does the Transylvanian Shore call Frankenstein?
The "Stitch-uation"!

What do you get by crossing an actor that played Dracula and an ad executive?
Bela "Logo-si"!

What kind of mafia will The Invisible Man, Darkman, and The Mummy want to form?

The "Gauze-a Nostra"!

What type of tattoo did Dracula's girlfriend get on her lower back?
A "Vamp Stamp"!

A Mummy's greatest fear is that no amount of gauze will cover their flaws.

Who is the Mummy's favorite actor from "Warlock"?
Julian "Sands"!

What kind of embalming fluid will transform Dr. Alan Jekyll into a monster?
"From-Al-To-Hyde"!

Why did the Jersey Shore bunch show up at Dr. Jekyll's place?
They were gonna tan his "Hyde"!!

What do you call it, if the Cohen brothers both changed into Dr. Jekyll's alter ego at the same time?
Two "Cohen's-Hyde"!

What landscaper turns into the Wolfman?
"Lawn" Chaney!

Did you know The Wolfman has a Facebook page?
Please go and "Lycan" it!

What moon phase turns The Wolfman into a silly creature?
A "Fool Moon"!

Speaking of that old flea bag, why is the Wolfman mad at his healthcare insurer?
They won't pay for his flea dips!

What kind of dog does the Phantom of the Opera have?
A "Candle-Labrador "Retriever!

The Hunchback of Notre Dame has a groovy cousin. What's his name?
Quasi-MOJO!

CHAPTER 7
STREET TRASH

Street Trash is a horror film directed by Jim Muro and written by Roy Frumkes. The story is that a liquor store owner finds a case of Viper, which he sells to the homeless for $1 a bottle. I like bargains, but the hooch makes the people melt!! Especially while on the toilet!

Hey kids, drinking Viper and the bathroom don't mix! Anyway, I hope to melt your funny bones with some awful jokes! The *Street Trash* toilet scenes give a whole different perspective to the phrase "Melting Pot."

What was the Street Trash wino charged with?
A DWM: Drinking While Melting!

Unaware of the upcoming irony, what 80's song did a *Street Trash* wino sing while on the toilet, drinking Viper?
"Melt With You"!

What were the winos saying about the liquor store owner selling the $1.00 bottles of Viper?
He who dealt it, "melt" it!

If you cross a religious-based musical and *Street Trash*, what would you get?
"Street Trash & The Amazing Technicolor Melting Winos"!!

What Swiss avant-garde artist helped design the *Street Trash* prop toilets?
"Rhoto Reuter"!

What do you get by crossing *Street Trash* with a Tennessee Williams film about Stella, Blanche and Stanley?
"A Street Trash Named Desire!"

What's the "Street Trash" hand in a Poker game? Royal Flush!!

What epic do you get by crossing Owen Wilson, Vince Vaughn and melting winos?

"Wedding Street Trashers!"

What invention helps the melting folks keep proper form in the bathroom?
"SQUATTER Potty!"

Street Trash is a tale of melting people.
"Skeet Trash" is a tale of actor Skeet Ulrich melting down from the paparazzi!

What musician melted into the toilet?
"LOO Reed!"

Which Native American helped create the plumbing sets of *Street Trash*?
"Running Toilet!"

CHAPTER 8
KAIJU!
GOD(ZILLA) BLESS YOU!

Kaiju are extremely large creatures. Think Godzilla, Mothra or Rodan, for example. You know, something really tall, like the teased up over-sprayed hair of a 1980's chick! Okay, maybe not that tall.

Is it possible to poke fun of these strange behemoths and not get buried under Monster Island? I'm willing to take that chance! If anything happens, it was Igor's fault.

What would happen if Gamera died? He'd stiffen up with "Rigor-Tortoise"!

What does a giant flying turtle have to do with photography?
You look through the "Gamera" eye!

What happens if Gamera puts a finger in an electrical outlet?
He gets "Shell-Shocked"!

What show gets great ratings on Monster Island?
My MOTHRA, the Car!!

Who is Gamera's favorite writer?
Mary "Shell-y"!

How do most arguments on Monster Island start?
Godzilla usually says, "Your MOTHRA is so ugly..."

Where does Gamera buy his gas?
At a "Shell" station!

What do you get by crossing Godzilla with Jay-Z?
A RAPtile!

Why is Gamera upset?
With all of the fighting he does, he feels he should be referred to as the original "Mutant Ninja Turtle"!

What's Gamera's favorite TV show?
The Mary "Turtle" Moore!

What Toto song does Gamera despise?
"Rodan-na"!

King Ghidora is thankful that he and his three heads escaped a fate like that of the Human Centipede.
They'd be the scourge of Monster Island.

What song by the 80's band, The Fixx, is about King Ghidora?
Saved by Monster Zero!

CHAPTER 9
TROG

Trog is a Joan Crawford movie about a monster. No, she's NOT the monster! It's a Caveman, or Troglodyte, they found and revived. They teach him fun games, like "fetch" and other things you would do with other pets. Or Snooky! Anyway, let's get our Hypoguns and take aim at *Trog*!

What do you get by crossing the tyrannical commissioner from *The Dukes of Hazzard* with a revived Troglodyte?
"Boss Trog"!

What brand of men's trench coats does Trog wear?
"London Trog", of corpse!

What do you get by crossing a 1970 Joan Crawford/Michael Gough film about a prehistoric Troglodyte and a child's jumping game?
Leap Trog!

What video arcade game is centered around a Troglodyte trying to cross a busy road in between traffic?
"Trog-ger"!

What favorite singer of Trog's did the "Fame Monster" album?
Lady "Trog-ga"!

Based on rock groups such as Rush, Yes, and Genesis, what kind of music does Trog like?
"Trog-ressive" Rock!

What happened when Trog had amnesia?
He didn't have the "Troggiest" idea who he was!

There was an underwater *Trog* sequel in the works. Its female star was Joan CRAWFISH!

What do you get when you cross a Caveman with a wooden shoe dance?
"TROGGING!"

When does the Caveman determine the weather for the next six weeks?
"Ground Trog Day!"

How did the Caveman fix the plumbing?
He "un-TROGGED" the drain!

Where did the Caveman get his spiffy shirts?
An L. L. Bean" CataTROG!"

What kids show starred a Caveman who asked, "Won't you be my neighbor?"
"Mr. TROGGER'S Neighborhood!"

The scientists booked their Caveman on *The Tonight Show*.
He was scheduled after the "MonoTROG."

What brand of pancake syrup does Trog like?
TROG Cabin Syrup!

CHAPTER 10
FACES OF DEATH

Faces of Death is a grisly, gruesome series of documentaries by John A. Schwartz. Almost as gruesome as any of the "Houswives of..." series!! The films are notorious and have been banned in many countries, much like my jokes! So, without further ado, let's do some jokes on the documentaries...

What documentary do you get by combining multiple desserts with loads of chocolate and multiple realistic deaths?
Faces of Death by Chocolate!

What do you get by crossing a play written by Arthur Miller and a documentary about the gruesome moments of death?
Faces of Death by a Salesman!

I heard there was a scene that shows Tony Shalhoub's brains getting eaten. Yes, they were noshing on Monk's brains. Oh, I think I got that slightly wrong. Oh dear. Never mind.

What do you get by crossing a Charles Bronson revenge film with a macabre documentary about death?
Faces of Death Wish

What documentary is about lopsided votes that result in death?
Faces of Death by a Landslide!

Is it true that in *Faces of Death* a man gives an electric performance, even while sitting? Ugh. That was bad.

What dark documentary is about a film with Goldie Hawn, Bruce Willis and Meryl Streep?
Faces of Death Becomes Her!

What do you get by crossing an intrinsic indie band with a death documentary?
Faces of Death Cab for Cutie

What you get by crossing a dark comedy with Edward Norton and a documentary about the moment of death?
Faces of Death to Smoochie!

What horror documentary series shows many deaths by a Moroccan style hat?
Fezzes of Death

Hear about the documentary about small groups of words?
It's called, "Phrases of Death!"

What do you get by crossing a KISS song and a gonzo documentary?
"Faces of BETH!"

What do you get by crossing a notorious documentary and Connie Seleca's husband?
"Faces of TESH!"

Hear about the strange Audrey Hepburn documentary?
It's called "Funny Faces of Death!"

Hear about the documentary series that looks at deadly power outages?
It's called "FUSES of Death!"

How many volts, go through the neck-bolts of the one called Frankenstein? He has no count of the exact amount. But, they sure make him feel fine.

The Six MINION Dollar Man!

What jiggly alien used to be NBC's sports anchor?
"Blob" Costas!

What do you get by crossing Dr. Zaus and a crowbar?

A PRY-mate!

What do you get by crossing an 80's doll and a Wes Craven voodoo film?
The Serpent and the Rainbow Brite!

What was the initial budget for *The Running Man* movie?

5K!

What's The Wolfman's favorite Irish song lyric?

"H-A-I-R-Y, A-G-A-I-N" spells "Hairy Again"!

Cross an Irish *Street Trash* wino and a hot sandwich, what do you get?
A "Potty Melt"!

What martial arts disco song does the Phantom of the Opera like?

Kung FUGUE Fighting! Man, those cats were fast as lightning.

What do you get by crossing a 1970 Joan Crawford/Michael Gough film about a prehistoric Troglodyte and a child's jumping game?

Leap Trog!!

What horror documentary series shows many deaths by a Moroccan style hat?

Fezzes of Death

"Fezzes" of Death!

Larry King Kong!

What's a Scream Queen's favorite algebra problem?

A "Linnea" Equation!

What do you get by crossing a Japanese cartoon kitten and a 1980's horror movie about a chainsaw-toting meat-making farmer?

Motel Hell-o Kitty!

KRAKEN a safe...

CHAPTER 11
RETURN OF THE LIVING DEAD

Return of the Living Dead is the first sequel to *Night of the Living Dead*, and it's a great mixture of horror and comedy. Much like when I went to my first junior high dance. There's crazy Zombies, punk rockers, a half Zombie, a Zombie called Tarman, a doomed couple of workers. This one brings a tear to the eye, as does cutting onions. But let's not waste away! Let's dig some jokes ...

Did you know the Zombies were Moonshiners?
They made "BRAIN alcohol!"

Those Zombies kept in the canisters might not be drunk, but they sure are PICKLED!

What game system does Tarman like?
"aTARi!"

Did you know the Zombie woman they interviewed in the film, did things in "HALF measure?"

What brand of shampoo did Tina use?
"I Can Smell Your Brains!" And boy did it drive her boyfriend, now turned Zombie, crazy!

What movie is a sequel about Zombies with hay fever?
The Return of the "Sniffling" Dead!

What condiment do the Zombies want to add to their tasty meals of punk rocker brains?
"Gray Matter Poupon"!

"Tarman" from *Return of the Living Dead* has an Italian folk song dancing cousin.
What's his name?
Tar-antella Man!

Who is Tarman's favorite actress?
"Tar-a" Reid!

What's Tarman's favorite song?
"Tar-ara Boom De-Yay"!

What's Tarman's favorite Christmas song?
"Win-Tar Wonderland"!

How does Tarman like his brains prepared?
"Tar-Tar"

Where does the private plane land?
The Tar-mac!

What college basketball team did Tarman try out for?
The North Carolina "Tar-Heels"!

CHAPTER 12
MOTEL HELL

Motel Hell is a film directed by Kevin Connor and it tells the tale of Farmer Vincent and his sister Ida, who take unsuspecting travelers and turn them into Farmer Vincent's Fritters! Now that you have an appetite, let's fatten up with some jokes!

What 1980's horror film is about a pig-head-wearing farmer that makes meat out of Motorola cell phone salespeople?
Motel Hell-o Moto!

They say gardening does a body good.
Unless you're in Farmer Vincent's body garden!

What do you get by crossing an AC/DC song with a 1980's horror film about Farmer Vincent and his sister, Ida?
Motel Hell's Bells!

What do you get by crossing a Barbara Streisand musical and a horror film about Farmer Vincent and his sister, Ida?
Motel Hell-o Dolly!

What do you get by crossing a 1980's horror film about murderous meat making farmers and the computer from *2001: A Space Odyssey*?
Motel "Hal"!

Farmer Vincent literally appeared pig-headed with a chain saw, even when it came to protecting his secret recipe.

If the motto is: "It takes all kinds of critters to make Farmer Vincent's Fritters," what does Farmer Vincent say about social networking?
"It takes all kinds of tweets, I figure, to make Farmer Vincent's Twitter."

Did you hear about "MOO-tel Hell?"
It's "COW-sing" a ruckus!

Did you know that Farmer Vincent wrote Renaissance music?
He calls it "MOTET Hell!"

Where could you get a room and have an extreme time?
"Motel HELLA!"

What framework lodging place did Farmer Vincent own?
"Motel HULL!"

What's Farmer Vincent's place for folks who are hard of hearing?
"Motel YELL!!"

CHAPTER 13
MISCELLANEOUS HORROR

Let's start this debacle of a chapter with the Superbowl.

Witnessing the Superbowl proved that Mutants, Monsters and Creatures do indeed exist.
Need proof? The Black Eyed Peas... 'Nuff Said!

What penalty did the "Poultrygeist" football team get?
Personal "Fowl"!

Don't tackle Jason Voorhees too high, because you might commit a... "face mask" personal foul.

Know who has the best "squares" today or any day? Pinhead, the Cenobite! He seems to "nail" it every time!

What kind of faith and hope football pass does The Wolfman throw?
A "Hair Mary"!

If a Rutger Hauer-looking "Hobo" ran the offense, what formation would he use?
"Shotgun"!

Why wouldn't The Thing (Fantastic 4) make a good wide receiver?

He's got "stone hands"!!

What penalty did Sweeney Todd get called for? Clipping!

When sung to an elephant, The Black Eyed Peas' lyric, "What you gonna do with all that junk in your TRUNK" has a way different meaning.

Perhaps the strangest thing I saw during the Superbowl was Slash from Guns & Roses rising from below the stage during The Black Eyed Peas performance.

My thoughts: They didn't plan on Slash being there. Maybe he was stuck under the stage from a previous show?

When Slash did rise, did he see his shadow? Did we get six more weeks of a drug and alcohol buzz?!

If Quint from *Jaws* has lunch with Bishop from *Aliens*... Do they go "halfsies" on the check?

Quint and Bishop both went to Tony Robbins for advice. He recommended they do some soul searching and give themselves a "gut check."

After what they went through, I think they need to do some gut searching first! You can't gut check if you can't find them!!

With that in mind...

Why does Hugh Laurie get nervous during certain scenes of *Aliens* or *Jaws*? He learned that a "House" divided, will not stand.

After his Alien Queen encounter, Bishop does not like the song lyric "Let's twist again"!

What Vincent Price/Peter Cushing film do you get by crossing the mag with Alfred E. Neuman and a Hugh Laurie TV show?
"MadHouse"!

What Paul Anka song should've been a theme song for The Thing with Two Heads?
"Put Your Heads On My Shoulder"!

What do you get by crossing a Keanu Reeves fantasy film with a winner that can see and do strange things we can't?
"ConstanSheen"!

How do you say "goodbye" in German, to a Vampire drinking Justin Bieber's blood?

"Auf Biebersvein"!!

What do you get when you cross Hugo Weaving's Matrix character and a green tart apple?
An "Agent Granny Smith" Apple!

What did the female ghost apply to her eyelashes? "Ma-Scare-a"!

What kind of commute involves a water tank, The Creature from the Black Lagoon, Aquaman, Jaws and Spongebob?
Car "Pooling"!

Why did Jaws laugh after eating too many scuba divers?
They gave him "Diver-tickle-itis"!

What do you get by crossing the song "Midnight Train" by Gladys Knight and a Clive Barker film?
"The Midnight Meat Train"!

Did you hear about the new KFC deep-fried Werewolf?
It's finger "Lycan" good!

What do you get by crossing a Leonardo Da Vinci painting and a William Peter Blatty novel?
The "Mona Legion"!

What horror film do you get by crossing a Matt Damon/Damon Wayans film fest with a Linnea Quigley film?
"Night of the Damons"!

What do you get by crossing *The Day of The Triffids* with *The China Syndrome*?
A Power Plant!

What Joe Dante film do you get by crossing the Buffy the Vampire character "Clem" with Rin Tin Tin?
"Clem-Rins"! (ugh!) Don't feed those after midnight!

What song from Walt Disney's Cinderella do ghosts like?
"Bippity, Boppity, BOO"!

What cheesy aftershave do Zombies like?
"Hai Ka-Rot-e"!

Rubik's Cube is a square puzzle. Kubrick's "Rube" is the puzzling square of a neighbor of the director of *The Shining*.

I want to thank the director of *Rubber* (a film about a killer tire) for trying to keep it "wheel".

Why did the cannibal cook take a pot of water to Susan from *Britain's Got Talent*?
He thought the cookbook said: Bring water to a "Boyle"!

What did the ski-masked killer from The Toolbox Murders do in the army?
He was a "Drill" Sergeant!

What do you get by crossing Porky Pig with Damien Thorne?
"Devilled Ham"!

What do you get when you cross "Rosebud" from *Citizen Kane* and ex-Federal Machete?
"Masleddy"!! (Ugh! That hurts!)

If Dan likes sitting at a table with werewolves, what Kevin Costner film does this remind you of?
"Dan sits with wolves"!

What root vegetable do you get by crossing a golfer and a cutting motion?
"Par-snips"!!!

In the 3D redo of *The Empire Strikes Back*, why is Jimmy Dean on planet Hoth, hosting Darth Vader?
To show Southern "HOTHspitality"!

Why did the ghoul put a small noose on his finger? He had a "hang-nail"!

What supplement made the robot so muscular? "Metal-bot-ic" steroids!

This is "hot" off the press: What actress will be in a remake of *Spontaneous Combustion*?

"Burn-adette Peters"!!

A monster got a job as a greeter. Without training, he "abruptly" greeted as "quickly" as he could.
He's called-"Greets Lightning!"

What do you get when you cross an old Tanya Tucker song with a George A. Romero Zombie film?
"The Delta Dawn of the Dead"!

Thing, from the Fantastic 4, has a hard time finding greeting cards that express his "sediments".

Why did The Incredible Shrinking Man go to med school?
To learn about "Micro" surgery!

What do you get by crossing Apple's tablet computer with an apartment for a Cyclops?
An "Eye-pad"!

What historical female monster protested by riding her horse while naked?
"Lady Ghoul-Diva"!

Why did the monster search for two identical potatoes?
He wanted to serve "matched potatoes!"

What method of protest do you get by crossing a David Bowie Vampire film while knocking down 10 bowling pins at once?
A "Hunger Strike"!

Radioactive is to Godzilla as Ratioactive is to Mathematicians.

Here's a *Star Wars* (film) - *Dallas* (TV) connection you never heard before.
Shot down: X Wing, Y Wing, J.R. Ewing

Where does food go when it dies?
To the "Mor-chew-ary"!

Do gravediggers like the Sugar Smacks cereal frog mascot?
Yes, in fact they "Dig 'Em"!

What do you call Michael Myers on the Love Boat? "Ship-Shape"!

What punctuation does Hannibal Lecter use to write something exactly as he heard it?
"Quid Pro Quotation Marks"!

What did Count Dracula, Count Dooku & Count Chocula do in the summers of their youth?
They were "Camp Count-selors"!

What kind of patterned socks do monsters like?! "Arrrrrrgggghhhyle Socks"!

What shape do monsters like?
"Rraagghhmbus"!!

Hear about the gravedigger ambassador? He was a "DIGnitary"!

What shape is loved by the Torture Chamber Master?
A "RACKtangle"! (That was a stretch)

What shape is loved by a Cyclops?
An "EYEsosceles Triangle"!

What film do you get when you cross flesh-eating plants, import tax and ego?
"Day of the Tarrif-ids"!

In *The Matrix Reloaded*, if Mitt Romney was like Agent Smith, attacking Neo in waves: What would Neo say?
Get yer "Mitts" off of me!

What do you get when you cross Bigfoot and a sod farm?
"Sodsquatch"!

After one bite of Iggy Pop, why did the Zombie spit the rest of him out?
He tasted too "Punky"!

If Choptop pours 2 gin & tonics on the metal plate on his skull, what geological formation does he claim to have?
"The Two-tonic Plate"

What song by The Pretenders do shapeshifters like? "Back on the Change-gang"!

What Adam Green film is about a hairstyle searching for enlightenment?
"Fro-Zen"! (Ugh!)

What do you get, if you cross a Michael Douglas romantic comedy with a stone Gargoyle?
"Romancing the Stone!"

What Gloria Gaynor disco song did the Cyclops like? "Eye" Will Survive!

Why do I protect my Raymond Burr statues (made by Tim) from the cold air?
So I don't "Shiver Me Tim-Burrs"!

What film do you get by crossing the Travelocity spokesman and a nightly demonic entity?
"Para-Gnome-al Activity"!

What song do you get by crossing a Clive Barker series & The Monotones?
"Who Wrote the Books of Blood"!

What main character do you get by crossing the film *Psycho* with Vikings?
"Norseman Bates"!

What Edgar Allen mixture of flowers and herbs gives you that "Pit and the Pendulum" scent?
"Poe-purri'"!

The Fly is turning to bodybuilding. He's staying away from steroids, so he'll be all "Gnatural"!

While at an auction, what did Twiki the robot say that caused trouble for Buck Rogers?
"Bid e Bid e Bid e Bid e Bid"!!

What do you get by crossing a 1982 Philippe Mora film and sounds from Dick Cheney's pacemaker?
"The Beeps Within"!

When Ripley was destroying the Alien Queen's eggs, what cooking utensil did she resemble?
An "Eggbeater"!

A Lycanthrope is a Werewolf. A "Nikeanthrope" is a Werewolf that changes when it sees the swoosh logo on sneakers.

What do you get by crossing the author of Naked Lunch and a loan officer?
William S. "Borrows"!

What film did The Incredible Shrinking Man think was about his opinion of girl's fashion dolls?
"Shrimp on the Barbie"!

What's the name of the flamboyant Vegas-based piano playing Zombie?
"LibeROTce"!!

What alcohol does a Russian Zombie drink?
"ROTka"!

What's a Zombie's favorite mountain range?
The "ColoROTo ROTties"!

What's a Zombie's favorite B-52's song?
"ROT Lobster!"

What kind of puzzle books do Zombies like?
"Connect the ROTs!"

What do you get when you cross the walking dead and a French cheese?
A "ZomBRIE"!

What lullaby do Zombie parents sing to Zombie babies?
"ROT-a-bye Zombie, on the grave top"!

If a vegetarian Zombie wants more fiber, what does he eat?
"LEGumes"!

What Toy Story character does The Fly like?
"Buzz" Lightyear!

Hear about Hanna-Barbera's reptile/Arnold Schwarzenegger cyborg movie?
Get ready for: The TermiGATOR!

If the Toxic Avenger gets a concussion, is that considered:
"Head Troma"?!

What does The Crawling Hand wear for orthopedic support that projects a tough guy look?
Brass Knuckles!

What was the name of The Melting Man's dog? "Puddles"!

When the Melting Man was a kid, people thought he was a real "Drip".

M&M's claim to "Melt in your mouth, not in your hands"... How does that work if The Melting Man wants some?

What song will the Pointer Sisters release after seeing *Tron: Trilogy*?
The New Tron Dance!

What film producer also invented an exercise device for your abs, back and torso?
Roger Core-man!

What 80's style pants/shorts combo, do monsters like to wear?
"Ghoulots!"

What Stan Lee/Marvel Comics monster will you get by crossing Jaws, Dracula, The Foo Fighters and the letter M?
"Fin Fang FooM"!

What reality show does Cujo like?
"Dog": The Bounty Hunter!

Why did the starving flesh eating virus want to get attached to Pinhead the Cenobite?

After seeing the grid work on Pinhead's face and skull he figured he could finally get three "squares" a day!

What sci-fi/horror film title could be the title of George Hamilton's biography?
"The Hideous Sun Demon"!

What do you get if you cross George Hamilton and the 1959 sci-fi/horror film, The Manster?
The "Tan-ster"!

What is George Hamilton's favorite musical overture by Wagner?
"TAN-hauser"!

What's the slogan of Devil-worshiping wheat gluten eaters?!
Hail "Seitan"!

What song by Wham is about a whispering ghost who just couldn't terrorize people anymore?
"Scare-less" Whisper!

According to a survey of exorcists, what type of nouns do demons like to use?
"Possessive" Nouns!

What do you get by crossing an 80's band and Japanese monsters singing, "Hush, hush. Shy, shy. Hush, hush. Eye to eye"?
"KAIJUgoogoo"!

Which 1980's actress was the coroner fond of?
"MORGUE-an" Fairchild!

What's a hangman's favorite Wilson Pickett song?
"Must Hang Sally"!

What do you get by crossing an H.G. Lewis film and a Nintendo gaming system?
The Wii-zard of Gore!!

A Zombie crawled out of his grave and had a song stuck in his head. It was "Rotten Top", by The Nitty Gritty "Dirt" Band!!

The Karate Kid was watching House of Wax when the power flickered on and off. He saw bits of it in between. It was truly "Wax on, Wax off"!

Funnier chemical-riddled landscape: Tromaville or Charlie Sheen?
Mine is on Tromaville. What say you?

What kind of meat does Freddy Krueger serve at dinner?
"Hand carved"!

How are plumbers and Vampires alike?
They know a lot about "drainage"!

You know what they say about "The Cat People"? They tend to "pussyfoot" around

What title do you get if you cross a book by Erich Remarque and a Yul Brynner sci-fi film?
"All Quiet on the Westworld Front"!

What kind of words do the giant creatures from *Them*! like?
"Ant-onyms"!!

What lyric do you get if Bobby Vinton sings about a ghost?
You are my "Spectral" angel!

What Motörhead song do grave diggers like?
Ace of "Spades"!

What prank do gravediggers like?
Ding-Dong "Ditch"!

What Dario Argento film do you get if a newcomer to a ballet academy discovers the residents are secretly making soap?
"Sudspira"!

A crematorium schedule has urn maintenance notes.
Thurs.urn 1, Fri.urn 2

What scifi film, with Kirk Douglas and Farah Fawcett, does the next day's note remind you of?
"Sat.urn 3"!

What kind of demon do you get by crossing a tattoo, a female sheep, and a school bus?
An "Ink-Ewe-Bus"

What kind of singing group is Sweeney Todd in?
A Barbershop "Goretet"!!

What do you get if you cross a Vincent Price film with an antiquated term to describe women in the Army?
"House of W.A.C.S"!

What do you get by crossing a Roddy McDowell film and a film with cowboys and dinosaurs?
"How Green Is My Valley of The Gwangi"!

In what Stephen King-based film do the children attack the adults on St. Patrick's Day?
"Children of the Corned Beef and Cabbage"!

What do Irish scifi-fans wear on St. Patrick's Day? "The 'Green' Slime"!

What song based on a film directed by George A. Romero and Dario Argento do you sing on St. Patrick's Day?
"When Two Evil Eyes Are Smiling"!

What plant symbolizes "good luck" to an Irish Zombie?
A "ShamRot"!!

What character portrayed by Stacy Keach is loved by the killer from *The Toolbox Murders*?
Mike "Hammer"!

What song do you get if you cross Vampires with the theme to "Mike Hammer"?
Harlem "NECKturne"!

If little children play "tag", then what do little Coroners play?
Toe "Tag"!!

What Sinatra song should be used in "The Cask of Amontillado," while Montresor imprisons Fortunato?
"I'll Be Sealing You"!

Why did the Vampire hunter buy a rifle scope?
To catch Vampires in the "Cross-hairs"!

What radio station does a monster listen to? NPArrgghh!

After watching the drill death scene in *City of the Living Dead*, I wondered if Bob had anything going through his head at that moment.

What do you call a "negative" written error at a blood bank?
A "Type-O"!

Where do little morticians learn their ABC's and 123's?
"Grave School"!

What Drifters song is loved by the Star Trek cybernetic villains who say "resistance is futile"?
Under The "Borg-walk"!

In *Star Wars*, which Wookie was a Greek pastry chef?
"Chew-baklava"! (Ugh! That was putrid!)

What do you get by crossing a Burt Reynolds thriller and *Terminator 3*?
"T3: Rise of Sharky's Machine"

If you cross the song "Live & Let Die", a zodiac sign, and a nickname for Jerry Garcia's band, you get this George A. Romero horror film:
"Die Aries of the Dead"!

Knowing that beans are indeed the musical fruit, after eating them, the lead person of the Human Centipede would turn to the other two, and say: "Get ready, because you will literally face the music"!

What film do Zombies think is about their version of an "Everlasting Gobstopper"?
"The Brain That Wouldn't Die"!

If the band Styx had a lyric for Vlad the Impaler, the first Vampire... Impale away, impale away, impale away with me, Vlad!

What do Frankenhooker and the monkey from *Raiders of the Lost Ark* have in common?
Both had "dates" that didn't end well!

If "Thomas the Engine" and "The Little Engine That Could" were monsters, would they come from "Trains-ylvania"?!

What do you get by crossing a Billy Crystal film at a cowboy camp and a horror film with Himalayan yogurt?
Slime City Slickers!

What kind of film do you get when crossing the Bourne series of films with *Saw*, *Hostel*, and other films like it?
  "Torture Bourne"!

CHAPTER 14
MISCELLANEOUS JOKES

What newspaper page do you get by crossing Iron Maiden's mascot, Tori Spelling, Al Gore and Led Zeppelin's guitarist?
"The Eddie-Tori-Al-Page"!

How do they serve pasta at "The Inferno"?
Al "Dante!"

They say zeitgeist means "spirit of the age". They also say "zitgeist", means "spirit of the acne."

If they made two clones of Cher and made sure to give her traits to each equally, this is the appropriate phrase that describes it: "Two Cher and Cher alike"!

What do you get by crossing the actor who played Jack Bauer and tiny tree-living cookie makers?
The "Kiefler Elves"

What do you get by crossing a medicated powder and a British spy?
"Bond. James Gold Bond"!

What do you get by crossing a Telly Savalas TV character and a French oceanographer named Cousteau?
"KoJacques"!!

What do you get by crossing a Madonna song and a piece of furniture?
"Chair-ish"!

After a "brush" with bad laws, a painter took "strokes" to "canvas" his neighborhood for petitions to get himself nominated for office.

What do you get by crossing the band that did "I Go Crazy" and an online video service?
"Flesh For Hulu"!

How does a German wheat-derived protein say "good day"?
"Gluten Tag"!

What do you call a refined, worldly prize fighter?
So-Fist-icated"!!

What does an oracle put on their waffles?
"SEER-up"

What does a Vampire oracle wear at formal occasions?
A "SEER-sucker Suit"!

Why did the FBI put Gregory Hines on the telephone lines?
To get a wire "tap"!

Cross these items: 5 digits of a human foot, hair from a horse's neck, two Hawaiian plants, and a canvas covering in front of a business. What sickness do you get?
"Toe-Mane-Pois-Awning"!

Eyeglasses with both near- and far-sighted lenses at the same time are called "Bifocals". Two enemies phoning you at the same time is called
"Bi-foe-calls"

What alcohol does a genie in a bottle drink?
"WISH-key"!

What do you get when you cross a Mark Twain story and a Madonna song?
"Pauper, Don't Preach"!

What do you get by crossing a Dr. Seuss story and a gangster's gun?
"The 'Gat' in the Hat"!

Why will a movie usher named Pat not allow you to re-enter the show, once you've gone out of the theater?
"When you've gone, Pat's the point of no return!"

What song lyric do you get by crossing Lon Chaney, Don Rickles, Jeff Bridges and a Michael Douglas film?
"Lon Don Bridges Falling Down"!!

What old school video game do snakes like to play?
"Asp-eroids"!

What do you call unscrupulous behavior between two video game arcade owners?
"Skull-DIGDUG-ery"!

A leaden sky does not mean heaven for dead pencils.

WE MUST PRESS ON!!! (Much like fake fingernails...) DON'T BE ALARMED!!! (Unless you're a clock...)

What song do you serenade your origami-loving girlfriend with?
"Paper Roses"!

Carpe Diem means "seize the day". For allergy sufferers it means "Sneeze the day"!

We know the rapper 50 Cent ("Fifty" Cent). Who is the rapper of choice for podiatrists?
"Footy Scent"!

What new Yoplait yogurt is just for hip hop fans? "YoPlaya"!!

What do you call an artist looking for a perfect drawing of the letter L in a pile of hate mail?
Looking for a "neat L" in a "Hate stack"!

What does a Lionel Richie song have in common with a proposed 24/7 all "Courtney Love" channel?
"Endless Love"!

What kind of interview do you get with James Bond's gadget man and The Fonz?
A "Q" and "Aayyyyyy" Session!!

Someday the polar ice cap may melt. Someday Amy Poehler's ice cap-pucino may melt, but chances are she'll drink it first.

What TV series do you get if Al Pacino is a detective in Hawaii, saying "Book 'em, Danno."?
"Hoowah Five-o"!

What do you get when you cross a dog and a Photoshop provider?
"Adobe-man Pinscher!"

Why did the brewery owner go to the doctor?
He had an "Ale-ment"!

What do you get when you cross a comedy club with an Eric Burdon and The Animals song?
House of the "Wry-Zing-Sun!"

"Synching" your phone means hooking it up to a computer. "Sinking" your phone means putting it on a boat with a hole in it.

What do you a computer programmer covered in lip balm from head to toe?
"Techno Salve-y"!

What does a prison inmate hope for, but a cell phone user hope against?
"No Bars"!

What does it mean if the Lone Ranger's horse hits you repeatedly in a consoling way?
Every "clout" has a "Silver" lining.

What boxing tournament did the spicy brown mustard enter?
"The Gulden's Gloves"!

Will Coca-Cola bring back the slogan "Have a Coke and a smile" to be used with Charlie Sheen?!
Not an "8 ball's" chance in Hell!

What fashion designer makes bullet resistant vests? "Kevlar Klein"!!

What Cherub from Netflix will bring you romantic films instantly on Valentine's Day?
"Queue-pid"!!

Hear about the guy who couldn't get "nuances"?
He couldn't get "nu-uncles" either. They were more than he could afford!

What do you get by combining the number 3.14, coffee drinks and an exercise regimen?
"Pi-lattes"!

For all of you peroxide blondes (shhh.... I won't tell). What's the name of Jim Croce song?
"If I Could Get Blonde from a Bottle", right?!

I'm wondering if Vanna White tries turning the letters on a Ouija board...

Tendrils of smoke filled... Wait a minute! Ten drills?! Heck that's enough to start up a hardware store!!
Yahoo!

A muscle fiber said to his brother: "Sinew" weren't home, I used the spare key and let myself in.

What do you get by crossing Charlie Sheen and Napoleon Dynamite's class president?
A Violent "Tor-Pedro" of truth!

If Elton John updated his lyrics to reflect technology... "Seems to me, I could live my life like a "Kindle" in the wind"

What kind of modeling clay did the singer, Sting, like as a kid?
PlayDoh-eeeeoeeeooyyaayyoooo!!

Larry Storch brought us TV's "F Troop". What troop does "The Jersey Shore" bring us?
"G.T.F. Troop!!

If you cross Nicholas Cage portraying a bee with a former Soviet intelligence service, what do you get?

The "Cage-y Bee"!

Why did the Gollum think Rosie O'Donnell had his "precious"?
According to a rhyme he heard Rosie had a "Ring" around her!

While working on a "tongue and groove" style floor, why did the carpenter consult with a heart surgeon, when he had the "tongue", but couldn't locate the "groove"?

Because according to his favorite Deee-Lite song: The "Groove" is in the heart.

What kind of thief can't stop stealing kelp by using their feet?
A "Kelp-Toe-Maniac"!

If someone in an airplane in the sky throws the "six Degrees of Kevin Bacon" game out the door, followed by Mr. Bacon, himself, what mythological point do you have?
Six Degrees between Kevin and Earth!

In the "Rime of the Ancient Mariner", the Mariner is said to have an albatross around his neck.
Not true. He ate the last sandwich of a shipmate who put him in a headlock, arms enclosing on his neck. His name was Albert Ross.

What positive thinking idea do you get when Jerry Mather of Leave it to Beaver has a Mime above his head?
"Mime over Mather"!

What do you get if you cross a Revolutionary War traitor with an anti-gas medicine?
"Beano-dict Arnold"!

What quote from *Superman 2* do you get if Neil Diamond walks into the room, followed by a bingo call and the villain who said it?
"Neil B4 Zod!"

What kind of party did they have at the archaeological site after finding a leg bone?
A "Shin-Dig"!

If you mix Michelle Kwan, Tom Cruise, a description of effervescence and Michael Biehn's *Aliens* character- what scientific math do you get?
"Kwan Tom Fizz Hicks!"

What would suggest Indiana Jones is from New Orleans?
There's bound to be an "Indy-Cajun" or two!

What do you get by crossing a Colin Firth film about a stuttering king and the nerd from *Saved by the Bell*?
"The King's Screech"!

What do you get by crossing Michael Jackson, a carved pumpkin and a piece of camping gear?
A "Jacko Lantern"!

Who is the female musician that has breathing problems while sleeping?
"Snore-y" Amos!

What blonde actress from the original 90210 likes horror films?
"Gore-y" Spelling

What do you call a caveman wandering along aimlessly?
A "Meander-thal"!

FrankenSTAN and Ollie!

Hear about the Hanna-Barbera reptile/Arnold Schwarzenegger cyborg movie?

Get ready for: The TermiGATOR!

Robocop is half man, half metal.
His hindquarters are recycled tea kettles.
Why was he frozen and inert?

He couldn't see or shut off his visor squirts!

Which strange life form has the worst face paint?
A) Killer Klown, B) Mimi, from The Drew Carey Show C) Gene Simmons

A) Killer Klown wants to eat you.
B) Mimi wants to date you.
C) Gene Simmons wants to merchandise you!

What do you get by crossing the author of Guerilla Warfare with Michael Meyers?

Shape Guevara

Count on It!

What punctuation mark is produced by the animators of *Nightmare Before Christmas*?

An "Ex-claymation point"!!

What do you get by crossing a perfume with a space invader?

Shali-MARS Attacks!

What Troma film is about white water rafting zombified grandmothers?
Rapids Grannies

What film has a giant boy with Frankenstein's heart leading a conga line worldwide?
Frankenstein Conga's the World!

What do you get, when you cross Snoopy with a Michael Keaton/Tim Burton ghost?

Beaglejuice, Beaglejuice, Beaglejuice!

The Frankenstein Coat of Arms

What men's cologne does the miner use?
"Pick-Axe" body spray!

Who is Robert's favorite male vocalist?
"Rubber" Goulet!

Danger Wool Robinson!

CHAPTER 15
MY SOUL TO TAKE 3D

My Soul to Take 3D is a Wes Craven horror film about a serial killer coming back to terrorize teens that share the same birthday. Plus, the birthdays are the date the killer was supposedly put to rest. I'm not sure, but I think I feel the need to write 12 Bad Jokes About: *My Soul to Take*. Mwhuhuhahahah!

What Wes Craven film has a hockey player arguing with a referee disallowing his goal?
"My Goal You Take"!

What Wes Craven film is about a baker confronting thieves?
"My Rolls You Take"!

What film do you get by crossing the new Wes Craven flick with the Chinatown sequel?
"My Soul Two Jakes"!

What horror film is about a bridge toll taker arguing with a penny-pincher that won't pay up?
"My Toll You Forsake"!

What film is about a mine owner telling workers to make big hunks of coal into little ones?
"My Coal You Break"!

What film is about a cereal maker describing how to produce his corn-based product?
"My Corn You Flake"!

What really scares the character "Bug"?
"Raid commercials"!

Do teens in Ripperton lie about their birthdays to get into bars?
No, because they're connected to the Ripper!

What Wes Craven film is about a grassy knoll full of leaves?
"My Knoll You Rake"!

What horror film is about a haunted shoe cobbler? "My Soles You Make"!

Who is "Bug's" favorite jazz singer?
"Gnat King Cole"!

What do you get when you cross a Wes Craven film and a Japanese soybean spread?
"Miso, You Paste"!

Ok, I confess those were absolutely dreadful! I hope you enjoyed them! Go see the movie, have a scare in 3D. Save me some popcorn. (Speaking of corn, these jokes are chock full of it!)

CHAPTER 16
BLACK SWAN

Black Swan is a drama/thriller movie starring Natalie Portman and is directed by Darren Aronofsky. In it, Natalie Portman's character lands the lead role in the ballet, Swan Lake. From that point, it's a downward spiral into madness.

I'll bet you didn't think ballet could be this fun, did you? Well, let's break out our leotards, and tutus, have a pirouette or two, as we tell:

What film do you get by crossing a Ridley Scott military film and a thriller about "Swan Lake"?
"Black Swan Down"!

What movie is about a ballet dancer demanding the studio floor has absolutely just the right finish?
"Shellac Swan"!

What ballet film has dancers performing in bullet proof jackets?
"Flack Swan"!

What Gino Vannelli song is being used in the Natalie Portman thriller, *Black Swan*?
"Black Swans Look Better in the Shade"!

If Natalie Portman's character was trying to earn a spot in a ballet version of "My Sharona", what would the film be called?
"The Knack Swan"!

What Natalie Portman thriller movie is about being terrorized by a castanets-playing ballet dancer?
"Clack Swan"!

What do you get by crossing the Indiana Jones archaeologist nemesis of *Raiders of the Lost Ark* and a dark ballet thriller?
"Belloq Swan"!

What movie thriller stars Daffy Duck as a tormented ballet dancer?
"Quack Swan"!

What do you get if you cross a thriller about "Swan Lake" and a Simon Pegg film about zombies?
"Black Swan of the Dead"!

What movie is about a ballet dancer built like a big truck?
"Mack" Swan!

Actress Rae Dawn Chong was so inspired by Black Swan, she's changing her name to: "B. Swan Chong"!

What do you get by crossing a Natalie Portman ballet thriller and a Sound garden song?
"Black Hole Swan"!

Well that was an allegro selection of jokes pertaining to the ballet thriller, *Black Swan*. I wouldn't recommend perusing the jokes in an adagio fashion.

I'm done with the knee bends and arm movements now. Plus, this leotard is itchy! I'm outta here! Oh, the things I do for you people! Ugh!

CHAPTER 17
INSIDIOUS

Insidious (2011) is a delightful haunting/possession film directed by James Wan. It's a film about a family and their attempts to prevent the suddenly comatose son from being possessed by spirits from a realm called "The Further".

You don't think that we could conjure up some bad jokes about this film, do you? In fact, I feel that I "possess" the tools and "spirit" to "further" us along to-
12 Bad Jokes About: *Insidious*

When Dalton, the little boy, goes up and falls down the attic ladder, it turns him off from playing "Chutes & Ladders" for good!

What movie is about Australian spirits trying to possess little Dalton?
"In-Sydney-ous"!

What film has possessed video game character Pitfall Harry stuck in a pit?
"In-Pit-ious"!

What do you get by crossing Insidious with a Frank Miller comic book film?
"Sin-City-ous"!

Even though the spirits are from "The Further", the one in the pictures with Dalton seems awfully near... Maybe they need to learn distance values?

What did Dalton from *Insidious* and Dalton from *Roadhouse* have in common? Everyone thought they'd be bigger!

What film has an acne-riddled spirit trying to possess Dalton?
"In-Zit-ious"!

Why did the spirits from "The Further" steal tents from a camping goods store?

They heard, incorrectly, that "possession" is "nine tents" of the law!

What movie is about *SNL* writers possessed by their comedy skits?
"In-Skit-ious"!

What film is about Kevin Federline trapped by the spirit of his possessive ex?
"In-Britney-ous"!

What movie had spirits in a "state of agitation"?
"In-Snit-ious"!

What was Dalton's least favorite Culture Club song that the spirits of "The Further" really liked?
"Coma" Chameleon!

Well that's what happens when I get horror films on my radar. I like to call it my "raduh", because of the jokes I'm prompted to write! Anyways, thanks to Insidious for being with us in "spirit"! (Ugh!)

CHAPTER 18
THE LAST EXORCISM

The Last Exorcism is about a minister reluctantly performing a spirit removal, or exorcism, in front of a film documentary crew. It's directed by Daniel Stamm and produced by Eli Roth, among others.

What did the minister do when his subject was possessed by the spirit of Charles Atlas?
Performed his "Last Flex-orcism"!

What do you call a procedure to remove the spirit of an Ogre, one final time?
The "Last Shreks-orcism"!

Every time the spirit took over, it would shake the victim, erasing their face. Soon, the features would appear line by line.
That called for the "Last Etch-a-Sketch-orcism"!

The spirit was very irritating and annoying.
So, they decided to have one: "Last Vexed-orcism"!

The minister knew the spirit to be an explosive type.
So, they had a "Blast Exorcism"!

What film has a minister trying to get rid of a fan of the U.S.S. Enterprise?
"The Last Treks-orcism"!

When the possession took place, the host would turn black or red, and yell "King Me!", over and over. So, they had to have a: "Last Checkers-cism"!

What film had a demonic possession that included nonstop singing of 80's tunes?
"The Last Retro-cism"!

What movie had a demonic possession that left everyone's hair full, shiny, and smelling good as if it were freshly shampooed?
"The Last Breck-corcism"!

What film had a minister trying to develop a cell phone application for exorcism?
"The Last Apps-orcism"!

What movie is about a minister removing a NASCAR racing spirit from a host, in a documentary?
"The Laps Exorcism"!

What movie has an exorcism drive-thru window, for your spirit removal needs on the fly?
"The Fast Exorcism"!

Ugh! I need an exorcism to rid my bad joke writing spirit! There you have it, 12 awful, wretched, bad jokes about *The Last Exorcism*!

CHAPTER 19
VAMPIRE GIRL VS. FRANKENSTEIN GIRL

Vampire Girl vs. Frankenstein Girl (2009) is an over-the-top gore-filled funfest, directed by Yoshihiro Nishimura and Naoyuki Tomomatsu. The film has a love triangle between Vampire Girl (Monami), Frankenstein Girl (Keiko), and Mizushima.

Throw in some satirical content about "the wrist-cutting society", some doo-wop songs and buckets and buckets of spraying blood, I must, nay—have to take a bite out of this film with... 12 Bad Jokes *About Vampire Girl vs. Frankenstein Girl*!

What's the name of the guy who created "Gumby" and Vampire Girl's power enabling "cloak"?
Art "Cloak-y"!

What song by The Kreeps did Frankenstein Girl's father sing to her as he put her together?
"Be My Frankenstein"!

What's Vampire Girl's favorite Al Pacino film?
"Sea of Blood"!

Monami once said her favorite 80's horror film was - "My Bloody Chocolate Valentine"!

Kenji Furano says: "Dicing" one's daughter is true happiness! But, thought better of an Andrew "Dice" Clay makeover and transformed her into Frankenstein Girl!

After eating a chocolate laced with Monami's vampiric blood, Mizushima thought the chocolate had some "bite" to it!

Who is the wrist-cutters' favorite guitarist?
Slash!

What is the wrist-cutter group's favorite heavy metal band?
"Wrist-ed" Sister!

What is the wrist-cutters' favorite Echo and The Bunnymen song?
"The Cutter"!

With the way Frankenstein Girl wielded her limbs as weapons, you could say she was: "Armed" and dangerous!

With her own arm screwed onto her head as a propeller, it's no wonder that Frankenstein Girl's favorite band is: "Propellerheads"!

What did Vampire Girl write in Frankenstein Girl's yearbook?
"Fangs" for the Memories!

Oh, brother! There you have it, Maniacs!

We poked some fun at a fun flick that has you on guard if you're offered chocolate from a mystery girl. Also, be on guard if your father is on the lookout for building better bodies! (Sheesh!)

CHAPTER 20
MY BLOODY VALENTINE

My Bloody Valentine was originally released in 1981 and directed by George Mihalka. It was remade in 3D and directed by Patrick Lussier in 2009. Either version will get your blood pumping!

The basic story is about miners who got trapped on the eve of the town's Valentine's Day dance. One of them resorted to cannibalism to survive and went on a killing spree, years later, after threats to the town to not celebrate Valentine's Day. The killer miner even went as far as removing the hearts of his victims with a pickaxe, placing them in a nice heart-shaped gift box. (Do I smell a Hallmark Cards moment?)

Oh, I won't be giving you flowers or sweets on February 14th, but, I will give you:
12 Bad Jokes about *My Bloody Valentine*! (With love, of corpse!)

What do you get when you cross a Charlie Brown film and a horror film about Valentine's Day?
Be My Bloody Valentine, Charlie Brown!

What do you get by having a tea named after Captain Bligh from Mutiny on the Bounty, crossed with My Bloody Valentine?
My "Bligh Tea" Valentine!

What horror film do you get by crossing a murderous miner and the "Orkin Man"?
"My Buggy Valentine"!

What Valentine's horror film has the drummer from Siouxsie & The Banshees?
"My 'Budgie' Valentine

What book like Hitler's *Mein Kampf* is the Killer miner planning to write?
"Mine Shaft"!

What horror film do you get if your tee shirt gift on February 14th has a "specific discolored stain"?
"My 'Blot Tee' Valentine"!

What horror film do you get if you cross the 1st syllable of Myspace, a British slang word, Jimmy Fallon's last name, and the prong of a fork?
"My Bloody Fallon Tine"!

The Murdering Miner was inspired by Carrot Top, a prop comic. So he took a freshly removed heart in each hand, smashed them together and said: "What Robert Wagner TV show does that remind you of?"
Heart to Heart!

What horror film do you get, by crossing a Carvel Ice Cream "whale character" cake with February 14th?
"My 'Fudgie' Valentine"!

Why did the murdering miner stuff a woman into a clothes dryer?
He overheard her say: "I wish I could go for a 'spin'"!

What's the pickaxe-murdering miner's favorite Nirvana song?
"Heart-Shaped Box"!

Well, there you have it! 12 deliciously awful jokes about a Valentine's horror movie! I'd recommend telling Cupid some of these, if you see him about!

CHAPTER 21
RUBBER

Rubber (2010) is a horror film directed by Quentin Dupieux. The unique villain Robert is a self-aware tire. Robert has telekinetic powers, although being a tire you could say he has "tele-pneumatic" powers.

He's on the rampage against a small desert town, bringing interesting ways of getting his "steel belted" points across! Is it "bias" that makes him "ply" his anger?

You'll have to see the film to find out! Until you do-here's 12 Bad Jokes about *Rubber* to "tire" you over...

Who is Robert's favorite male vocalist?
"Rubber" Goulet!

What type of holistic treatment scares Robert the tire?
"Acu-Puncture"!

What is Robert's favorite music industry magazine? "Spin" Magazine!

Who is Robert's favorite country singer?
Reba McEn-"Tire"!

Who is Robert's favorite actor?
"Tread" Williams!

What do you call Robert getting reincarnated into another tire?
"Retiring"!

What is Robert's favorite vacation destination? Buenos "Air-es"!

What type of food scares Robert the tire?
"Flat" Bread!

Who is Robert the tire's other favorite country singer?
LeAnn "Rims"!

What type of music does the tire listen to?
Anything up and down the "Radial" dial!

Why does Robert the tire workout?
To get "Pumped Up"!

What happened during an argument between Robert the Tire and the Sheriff?
They had a real "Blowout"!

Oh, Maniacs. To read these must give you such nausea. A headache maybe? A groan? Something? But here you have it, 12 bad jokes, time for the rubber to hit the road.

CHAPTER 22
SPLICE

Splice, directed by Vincenzo Natali, is a horror sci-fi film about rebellious scientists dangerously toying with DNA splicing and a being that is a result of those experiments.

Do you think there might be a joke or two about Splice written by Yours Drooly?! Of "Corpse!" In fact, here are 12 *Splice* Movie Jokes!

Who's Drens favorite comedian?
Andrew "Splice" Clay!

What's Dren's favorite all-girl singing group?
The "Splice" Girls!

What's Dren's favorite alternative group?
"Gene" Loves Jezebel!

Where do Elsa and Clive go for their combinations of seasonings?
The "Splice" rack!

What does Dren like to eat?
"Splices" of pizza!

Elsa and Clive have scientist competitors named Levi and Strauss; they patch together pieces of denim as a form of "Jean Splicing!"

Why did Else and Clive use different DNA sources?
Variety is the "splice" of life!

Why is Dren bald?
A Rasta took her hair to make "Dren-locks!"

What show did Dren want to see?
The "Splice" Capades!

What's Dren's favorite Vanilla Ice Song?
"Splice Splice Baby"!

What's Dren's favorite San Francisco treat?
Splice-a-Roni!!

What did Elsa and Clive get Dren for Father's Day?
A bottle of Old "Splice!"

Well, there you have it! 12 *Splice* Movie jokes. Hopefully, you had a barf bag nearby! The jokes are just awful!

CHAPTER 23
PIRANHA 3D

Piranha 3D was directed by Alexandre Aja, and was released in theaters during the summer of 2010.

It is the story of prehistoric man-eating fish getting set free by an underwater earthquake/tremor. A feeding frenzy is to follow, as the little things tear up some spring breakers on a lovely beach!

It stars Elisabeth Shue, Eli Roth, Ving Rhames, Christopher Lloyd, Richard Dreyfuss, and more…

Let's test the treacherous waters with 12 Bad jokes about *Piranha 3D*!

What do you get if you cross a 3D horror film about deadly fish tearing up humans and the legendary drummer from Rush tearing up the kit?
"Peart-ranha 3D"!

What 3D film is about skunk-fish terrorizing people filled beaches?
"Pew-ranha 3D"!

If this R&B artist asked you a favor in a memo it would be signed, "Pir-Rhianna"!

A sequel to *Piranha 3D* has the man-eating fish in Antarctica; it will be called "Brrrrrrranha 3D"!

If a Russian space station was in the shape of a deadly man-eating fish, you'd call it "Mir-anha"!

What *Piranha 3D* actor do you call to fix your circuit/breaker box at home?
Richard Drey-fuse!

The piranhas are big Abe Vigoda fans. What is their favorite Barney Miller character portrayed by him?
Fish!

What man-eating fish perspires and needs deodorant?
Sure-anhas!

What kind of deadly fish swim in nothing but filtered water systems?
A PUR-anha!

The piranhas are so fast they aren't seen easily. So, could you call them blur-anhas?

Elisabeth Shue is among the cast of Piranha 3D. Alistofbetsinhershoe was a numbers runner, and hid the tickets in her sneakers.

According to SAG, the little piranhas will be paid like their body covering... In "Scale"!

Ugh! Ohhh! Groan! Ack! Barf! These are the reactions those 12 bad jokes should have given you. We've dipped our toes in the waters and taken 12 bites out of *Piranha 3D!*

CHAPTER 24
SUPERHEROES AND CARTOONS

Superheroes are the crime fighting men and women that have their underwear on the outside of their clothes, while smashing criminals!!

My favorite Superhero is Batman, always has been. At my Great-Grandparents' Wedding Anniversary party, I sang Nanananananananananananananana-Batman!" with the band, led by my father and his brothers, as they played Neal Hefti's infamous theme song for me. I was really young, four or five.

I love Cartoons. The sillier, the better! Any Warner Brothers, MGM or Hanna Barbera short just makes my day! Here's some jokes to jumpstart your smiles...

Did you hear Catwoman went green?
She even changed her name to Selina KALE!!

Did you hear Batman's fight words had a baby?
It's a "BAM!bino"

How do you know if the Thing from the Fantastic Four isn't feeling well?
He looks a little Shale!

What is Aquaman's favorite song?
"You Trouta Know" by Atlantis Morissette!

What do you get if you cross Lamont Cranston and Homer Simpson?
The Sha-d'oh!

If Batman went vegan and wanted to rename name his Batusi dance, what would he call it?
"Batu-SOY!"

What do you get when you cross Porky Pig, a Robin Hood character, and a zombie?
The Sheriff of "Rotting-ham"!

Who is the Human Torch's favorite director?
Martin "SCORCH-ese!"

What do Pinocchio and Jimmy Durante have in common?
NOSE-riety!

What nightcap do they have at Arkham Asylum?
"Crème DEMENTIA!"

Why would you ask Plastic Man, Mr. Fantastic, or the Elongated Man to help you budget your money?
They know how to STRETCH a buck!

If Porky Pig gave his clothes to his younger siblings, would you call them "HAM Me Downs"?

What member of the Thundercats used to be a member of the Commodores?
LIONO Richie!

What's the favorite lunch meat of the Avenger Ant Man?
"PYM-ento Loaf!"

Why did the Human Torch go to the dentist? He had "SINGE-ivitis!"

What do you get when you cross a Batman villain and Angelina Jolie's father?
"Voightson Ivy!"

What's Pinocchio's favorite Beatles song?
Nose-wegian Wood!

What social networking site does the Justice League's sorcerer use?
Fates-Book!

What do you get when you cross the Flash's gorilla mastermind enemy and the King of Monsters?
Groddzilla!

What does Sylvester the Cat say after getting a bad tattoo?
"Sufferin' Suckytat!"

What's the name of Namor's Italian cousin?
The Sub-Marinara!

If Porky Pig has chimney issues, does that mean he has a "Swine Flue" problem?

If Spider-Man's villain Kraven portrayed Quasimodo, would you call it "The Huntsback of Notre Dame"?

Where do the Three Little Pigs and Big Bad Wolf get their news?
The Huff and Puffington Post!

What Batman villain do you get by crossing Jeff Spicoli and Herman Munster?
The PennGwynn

What do you get when you cross a Jack Kirby Fourth World escape artist and a salad dressing/ sandwich spread?
Mr. MiracleWhip!

Why did Bugs Bunny walk across Daffy Duck's beak when the waiter brought the check?
He wanted to "foot the bill"!

Where in jail did they put indie comic book bad boys Milk and Cheese?
Soli-dairy Confinement!

Why would Daffy Duck make a good detective?
He has "De-Duck-Tive" reasoning!

Did you hear Batman's fight words had a baby?
It's a "BAM-bino!!"

What do you get by crossing OO7
and Roger Corman's version of Mary Shelly's monster?

"Frankenstein UnBOND!"

How does Darry Vader get relief?
"A SITHS bath !"

What's the Phantom's favorite coffee drink?
La-la, la, la, la, la, la, la. LATTE!
Yeshhh. It makes him sing: "Soy, Latte, Do!"

Which Vancouver Canuck hails from Dr. Moreau's Island?

Dave TIGER Williams!

The Creature From the Black Lagoon, swims in most bodies of "drink."
He can't swim the Hudson River- it has everything, including the kitchen sink.

How does Maniac Cop order lunch?
He calls in an APB on a PBJ, BLT, BBQ and a V8

"The Scream, Blacula. The Scream."

OptiMOOSE Prime!

Sorry, TLC Channel. Your cake baking tyrant on his ear should be tossed. "Father's Day" from *Creepshow* had a better "Cake Boss"!

DABula!

What's The Mummy's favorite campfire song?

"Tomb-by-ya"!

Munster go Tiki

CHAPTER 25
ALIENS

Aliens is the sequel to *Alien*, and it follows Ripley on her return to LV-246, where she and a group of Marines find a little girl who survived an Alien attack. Waiting for them is a group of gooey Alien creatures and an egg laying Queen.

What Sigourney Weaver character had holes in her blue jeans?
"RIP-ley!!"

What plumber character was Sigourney Weaver supposed to play in the Alien franchise?
"DRIP-ley!"

What do you get by crossing the crab-like stage of the Alien and a member of the A-Team?
A FACE Hugger!

In *Aliens* Ripley confronts the Alien Queen and destroys her offspring. This makes the Queen very "EGG-ressive!"

How old is Bishop the android at the end of *Aliens*?
Not sure, but I think he measures it in "half" life!

What Beatles lyric did Bishop the android think of at the end of *Aliens?*
"Suddenly, I'm not HALF the man I used to be!"

When Ripley fought the Queen Alien, she stepped in a puddle of vinegar. Making her Power-loader a "SOUR-loader!"

What's the name of the little gassy colonist girl?
"POOT!!"

Why did Ripley and the Marines invade Nickelodeon?
They thought it was a "DOUG Hunt!"

Which version of the Xenomorphs liked to "crowd in" on people?
"Space Huggers!"

What do you call an Italian Alien?
A "GINO-morph!"

Which Alien is spotted at all of the hot night clubs?
A "SCENE-o-morph!"

Why was Ripley left for 57 years?
Her Uber driver had a few gigs and an Etsy store to close, first!

Which streaming service did the last colonist of LV-426 sell her story to?
"NEWTFLIX!"

What shop followed Sigourney Weaver from "Ghostbusters "to "Aliens "?
The "ZUULaco!"

CHAPTER 26
THE MANITOU

The Manitou is a tale of a 400-year-old evil medicine man named Misquamacus, who is resurrected and grows on the back of a psychic's girlfriend.

Who do you get by crossing the title characters from *Scarface* and *The Manitou?*
"Tony Manitou-ya!"

What's Manitou's least favorite Belinda Carlyle song?
"Circles Made of Sand"!

How does a 400-year-old medicine man "count off" a song?
"Mani-one, Manitou!"

The Manitou was growing in a tumor: A pod or pocket on a woman's back. He could cast spells. So... he was a "Podcaster?"

What do you get by crossing an actor from Emergency and a 400-year-old medicine man?
"Randolph Manitouth!!"

Who's the ultimate "backseat driver?"
The Manitou!!

What horror film about an evil medicine man has Tony Curtis and Dave Grohl?
"The Mani-Foo!"

What's a 400-year-old medicine man's favorite day of the week?
"Mani-Two for Tuesday!"

Misquamacus is 400 years old. He doesn't look a decade over 300!

The Manitou was mistaken for a beauty pageant contestant, what with the long hair and a name like "Miss Quamacus!"

The Manitou had a favorite Terminator quote, with a twist. He'd always say, "I'll be in the back."

Did you know Misquamacus auditioned for a sitcom?
Yeah, it was "Manitou and a Half Men."

What did they call Misquamacus when he couldn't stop overeating?
"The HAMitou!"

CHAPTER 27
SLIME CITY

Slime City is a horror movie directed by Greg Lamberson. It's the tale of an art student who gets a deadly mutant changeover, after eating some weird Himalayan yogurt and drinking wine with it. I didn't know such a pairing existed! You know what else exists? The Easter Bunny! No, no, after that. *Slime City* jokes!!

What soft drink do they drink in Slime City?
Sprite, because it's lemon/slime flavored!

What country singer is a favorite in Slime City? Leann Slimes!

What is a favorite Paul Simon song in Slime City? "Slip Slimin' Away"!

What objects hang in front of houses in Slime City that catch the wind and make noise?
Wind Slimes!

What game do they play in Slime City?
"Slimin' Says!"

Why did the Slime Head's every word bounce and repeat as if he were in a canyon?
He was full of "Echo-plasm!"

If Jamie Lee Curtis wants a life-changing yogurt, she should switch from Activia to Slime City Himalayan yogurt!

What do the Slime City citizens sing on Dec. 31st? "Auld Lang SLIME!"

Hear about the new Himalayan yogurt home improvement?
It gives you SLIMING glass doors!!

What happens if Goodfellas has Himalayan yogurt? Someone has to get their "Slime box!"

Hear about the "Slime City" Improv group?
They're called "The Not Ready For SLIME-time Players!"

What was the mantra of glop covered Slimeheads? What's Good for the GOOS is good for the gander!

Where do Slimeheads get their weather fix? "CLIME City!"

CHAPTER 28
DAYBREAKERS

Daybreakers (2009) is a vampire film noir hybrid with a futuristic vein (see what I did there?), starring Ethan Hawke, Sam Neil, and Willem Dafoe. It is directed by the Spierig brothers, Michael and Peter.

The film is about a human blood shortage affecting the vampires and the struggle to find a suitable replacement. It's quite stylish and entertaining. So there's ... wait. I think ... yes, there will be ...

Mwhuhuhuhahahahaha! 12 Bad Jokes About: *Daybreakers*

The film's opening sequence had a vampire girl facing a sunrise. Obviously, she forgot her sunscreen because she got so burnt! OMG!

Get yer ears on for this one, good buddies! What Ethan Hawke/Sam Neil movie involves vampiric truckers calling on C. B. radios?
Daybreakers, Breakers!

What film do you get by crossing a George Romero classic and a "vampires ruling the earth" film?
Daybreakers of the Dead!

The first test subject that received a blood substitute had an interesting last few words. He said, "Wow, this stuff blows my mind!" Unfortunately for him, it actually did. Really, in a bloody explosion!

What do you get by crossing an old sitcom with Valerie Bertinelli and a vampire film?
One Daybreaker at a Time!

Watching Ethan Hawke and his brother's characters fighting in *Daybreakers* makes me think that this is a real "blood-feud."

What vampire band do you get by crossing a flamboyant musician and his group from *Purple Rain* and *Daybreakers?*
Morris Daybreakers and the Time!

What vampire movie is about finding a blood supply for an actress from the 50's and 60's?
Doris Daybreakers!

Why is Jared the Subway pitchman angry?
Because Daybreakers used the term "Subwalk" to describe a series of well-kept tunnels for vampires. He thought he patented the phrase!

What Elvis lyric would describe Willem Dafoe's character getting stuck in the sunlight while still being a vampire?
Just a hunk, a hunk of burning love!

What Monkees song would go well with this film? Daybreakers Believer!

There's a deleted scene from the film's ending, where Ethan Hawke's character, now human, stops for donuts. How many did he get?
A Daybakers Dozen!!

Oh Brother. We raked this one over the coals. This film, that reminds us of *Gattaca*, but in a good way. Oh, why did we take 12 swings at it? Well, that's our job. It was an enjoyable film to watch and poke fun at. Oh, Maniacs. To read these must give you such nausea. A headache maybe? A groan? Something? Tune in soon, for more dreck! Take care!

CHAPTER 29
TROLL HUNTER

Troll Hunter (2010) is directed by Andre Ovredal and is the story of university students filming the exploits of a man named Otto, who is involved in a clandestine government group. The group secretly protects the people of Norway from giant Trolls. You know what?

I feel like investigating something myself. Let's see if we can put together a gigantic group of bad jokes! How about … 12 Bad Jokes About: Troll Hunter

Who do you call when giants hide your TV remote? ConTROLL Hunter!

What film is about searching for the lowest gas prices from the giant fuel companies?
PeTROLL Hunter!

Before Otto was hunting giant humanoids, he worked at a bakery tracking down missing goods. What did they call him?
ROLL Hunter!

Being an avid fan of fifties' music made Otto look for clubs that held specific sock hop dance nights. He was kind of a … STROLL Hunter!

What film is about a guy trying to find a pristine VHS of a John Buechler-directed horror film?
Troll Hunter!

What film is about finding a person that communicates with giants via low, guttural sounds?
Troll GRUNTER!

What film is about a gigantic football kicker?
Troll PUNTER!

What movie is about the search for a small train that shuttles around gigantic beings?
Troll SHUNTER!

What do you get by having a gigantic baseball- playing being not complete his swings at bat?
Troll BUNTER!

What film is about a man named Otto looking for incredibly large rolls of parchment?
SCROLL Hunter!

What movie is about a group of university students filming a search for giant highway collection booths?
TOLL Hunter!

What movie is about a man named Otto, searching for whimsical gigantic beings?
DROLL Hunter!

Well, we did it. Maniacs, we took a few giant steps towards a fun movie. Twelve bad joke steps to be exact. Hopefully, you weren't frightened, but enlightened! You must stop back, sometime soon, for the next batch of bad jokes! I'll be looking forward to it!

Mwhuhuhuhahahahaha!

CHAPTER 30
DEAD SNOW

The 2009 Norwegian horror/comedy film, *Dead Snow*, or *Dod Sno*, was directed by Tommy Wirkola. It centers on med students spending their spring break on a ski trip in a cabin... What they don't know is they are about to be attacked by Nazi zombies! (It could happen ...)

I love snow! I love zombies! Heck, I love movies that vilify Nazis! Let's get out our sleds and go downhill with: 12 *Dead Snow* Jokes!

What movie is about credit card collection agency Nazis in a snowy setting?
"Cred Snow"!

What do you get if you cross a Barney Rubble neighbor and a Norwegian horror flick?
"Fred Snow"!

If the last letter of the Canadian alphabet was in the snow chasing med students, you'd call it "Zed Snow"!

If the lead singer from Poison was attacking those that ventured into his snow-filled region, you could refer to it as "Brett Snow"!

Speaking of snowy regions, which movie has more snow, "Dead Snow" or "Scarface"?

If a zombiefied Kevin Federline was attacking the med students, is it Called "K-Fed Snow?!"

What natural cough drop do rigor mortis-stricken Nazi zombies use?
Rigor-la!

If the head of the *Beverly Hillbillies* family, the Clampetts, was hunting Nazi zombies in a horror film, would it be called "Jed Snow"?!

If the "Madman from Michigan" was running around snowy mountains, chasing zombies, and singing "Wango Tango", in a horror film, you'd probably title it "Ted Snow"!

With the premise being medical students taking spring break in the snow-covered mountains, you could call this horror film "Med Snow"!

What Norwegian horror film is about Rastafarian Nazi zombies and their hair? "Dread Snow"!

What film has bridezillas running after Nazi zombies in the snow? "Wed Snow"!

Well, there's 12 bad jokes about *Dead Snow*, a fun horror film!

We piled it on like an "avalanche." I mean, you've got to be able to "bank" on getting the "drift," and not "flake". (Ugh! That was bad!)

CHAPTER 31
HO! HO! HORROR!

It's the holiday season and there are horror films firmly in the spirit and theme of Christmas! Some even have remakes or sequels? Yes it's true (shudder!). Check out these titles: *Silent Night, Deadly Night; Black Christmas; Christmas Evil; Santa's Slay; Don't Open 'Till Christmas; Gremlins; Santa Klaws; To All a Good Night; Jack Frost; Rare Exports: A Christmas Tale*

As you can see, there's a fairly decent amount to choose from and poke fun at. So, let's have some Christmas-flavored horror film fun, with some deliriously bad jokes about them!

What "green" film do you get by crossing A Charlton Heston sci-fi film and a film with a killer dressed as Santa Claus?
"Soylent Night, Deadly Night!"

What movie is about creature rotary tools that multiply if you get water on them or feed them after midnight?
"Dremelins!"

What film is about a serial killer, reincarnated as a snowman that has emotional distress about everything?
"Jack Fraughts!"

What film is about a murderer, dressed as Santa Claus, who likes Bo Diddley music?
"Silent Night, Diddley Night!"

What film has an escaped maniacal dentist returning to his childhood home to prevent tooth decay?
"Plaque Christmas!"

What film has a killer in the form of a snowman cake?

"Jack Frosting"!

What film has a killer pretending to be Santa who can't stand anything on the E! Channel?
"Christmas E! full!"

What film has Tony Hawk dressed as Santa Claus, performing skateboard tricks under the Korvatunturi Mountains?
"Rare X-Sports"!

What film has a guy dressed as Santa, obsessed with a B-movie actress and her choice of instant coffee?
"Sanka Klaws!"

What film is about a killer targeting everyone dressed as Santa, coming for you next, as you go to your job as mall Santa?
"Done Hopin' 'Till Christmas!"

In what movie did a demon's son, serving 1000 years as Santa, finally have his gambling debt "wiped clean"?
Santa's "Slate"!

In what film does a Santa-costumed maniac torment finishing school girls by making them work out to Buns of Steel twice?
"Dual: A Glute Night"!

Ugh! I think this batch of bad jokes will land me on the naughty list, for sure! I hope you enjoyed them! Yeah, right!

CHAPTER 32
PROMETHEUS

Prometheus (2012) is the long-awaited film by Ridley Scott. This marks his return to the landscape he laid out in the movie *Alien* (1979). Space Jockeys, Charlize Theron, Noomi Rapace, and Xenomorphs, OH MY! Let's not waste time and blast off, into...12 Bad Jokes About: *Prometheus*

What did the crew forget to pack, but found, during their expedition?
Space Jockeys!!

What film is about having an alien lodged in your chest, making you reach for a Bromo Seltzer?
BROmetheus!

What film is about a space crew exploring the origins of an alien singing Sheryl Crow songs?
CROWmetheus!

I think Jon Taffer of Bar Rescue would lose his cool if he saw David stick his contaminated finger in a drink, then serve it!!

An Engineer and David both had theirs heads toted around in bags. If there were 6 more and a role by Joe Pesci, it could have been the prequel to *8 Heads in a Duffel Bag!*

What Ridley Scott film is about a space cowboy trying to make his horse, Metheus, stop?
WHOA, Metheus!

What film is about Frodo and his friends of Middle Earth exploring the start of mankind?
FROmetheus

After seeing the engineer down a mysterious drink, then immediately melt away, you know the execs at Trimspa had hope of a relaunch!

What film is about exploring space to discover the link to the author of The Raven?
POEmetheus!

What country music singer did the Prometheus crew like?
Waylon Yutani Jennings!

Why did the systems of David, the synthetic being, drastically slow down once a month?
Because AT&T throttled him for too much usage!

What movie deals with discovering links to an actress named Madeline, known for Last of the Mohicans, Bad Girls, and more?
STOWEmetheus!

Ugh!!! Oh Brother! We found 12 links (bad jokes, OF CORPSE!) to *Prometheus!*

Well, Weyland Industries wants to send me out on an excursion, to see if I can find a link to some humorous people!

Hey! I'm humorous, aren't I?! Hey...David, put down those eggs!

CHAPTER 33
HORROR WESTERNS

Ghoul Mourning, Maniacs!! Do westerns and horror films go together? More often than you would believe. Films like *Billy the Kid vs. Dracula, The Valley of Gwangi, Westworld, Ghost Town, Jonah Hex, Quick and the Undead, Jesse James Meets Frankenstein's Daughter*, and many more gave the weird connective base between rootin', tootin', gun slinging action and ghastliness, mixed with the supernatural.

Well, cowpokes. What do you think? Can we rustle up a few Bad Jokes about Horror Westerns? I reckon we can!!

Saddle up! Here we go! 12 Bad Jokes About: Horror Westerns

What western film stars Frankenstein, Clint Eastwood, and America Ferrera?
The Friend, Good. The Fire, Bad, and The Betty, Ugly!

What horror western film combines cowboys, dinosaurs, and salad dressing?
Hidden Valley of Gwangi!

What horror western crosses a giant mutant sheep, Native Americans, and tires without air?
Godmonster of Indian Flats!

What do you get by crossing an amusement park with robotic cowboys and nonstop rain?
WETsworld!

What film is about Dracula facing off against the Hostess Snack Cakes cowboy mascot?
Twinkie the Kid vs. Dracula!

What new horror western film do you get by crossing *The Burrowers* with creatures that attack you from under and within a chest of drawers?
The BUREAUers!

What film do you get by combining a phenomenon from *Highlander* and a zombie-filled horror western?
The Quickening and the Undead!

What remake of *Left for Dead* will have cowgirls on the run, hiding in a haunted, abandoned comedy club?
LAUGHED for Dead!

What weird horror western has Jesse James tripping and falling into the pet entrance at Frankenstein's kin's home?
Jesse James Meets Frankenstein's DOG DOOR!

What horror western is about a man named Jonah who invented a six-sided hand tool?
Jonah HEX Wrench!

What film is about an ongoing tennis back and forth, between cowboys and dinosaurs?
The VOLLEY of Gwangi!

What horror western combines the film *Mad at the Moon* and a story about a woman who changes into a football analyst during certain moon phases?
MADDEN at the Moon!

Yeeeeeee haaawwwww, Maniacs! We dang, done, did it!

Twelve lead slinging, spur jangling bad jokes!!

Take a bow! You done real good! Have yourselves a sarsaparilla or two! Quench yore thirst!

Okay! Okay! I'll stop. It's true, we made fun of some weird films; they deserved it! Honestly, they are entertaining. Go watch one and see for yourself! I dare you!

See you next time, Of Corpse!

CHAPTER 34
FINAL DESTINATION FILMS

The *Final Destination* series is directed by Steven Quale. Quale, along with previous directors James Wong, David R. Ellis (two *Final Destination* films each), brings an interesting idea to the screen.

Premonitions of death and cheating death itself are the common threads. Tony Todd takes another turn in his recurring role. The uncommon thread is the one we will weave with today. I'm talking about:

12 Bad Jokes About: The *Final Destination* Franchise

These people escaped disaster and death, because of a friend with premonitions. How were they chosen? Did they click "like" on Facebook for "If you want to escape disaster and death"? Sheesh!

What film is about LP records cheating death because of premonitions?
"Vinyl Destination"!

In *Final Destination 2*, one lucky (for a little while) guy wins the lottery. His appliances all explode in his apartment, forcing him out to his death! Dude, exploding appliances? That's what you get for going with "rent to own"!

What film is about a premonition of cheating a skin rash?
Final "Desitin-Nation"!

In *Final Destination 3*, there is a tanning bed death scene. If they had a premonition about "spray tanning," they could have avoided that "toasty" turn of events!

What film is about a place, that has endless supplies of CD's of an indie folk band, and DVD's of a 1930's western film series of the same name?
Final "Destry-Nation"!

In the fourth film, *The Final Destination*, there is a death by a flying tire: "Wheel-ly"?! Did we have to go there?

What film has a premonition about a death cheating, cleaning service?
Final "Dusty-Nation"!

In *Final Destination 5*, there is a scene of death by acupuncture. Hmmm… I'm thinking that "Stuck on You" by Lionel Richie would not be an app-ropriate musical selection at that time.

What film has a premonition of drinking some good alcoholic beverages?
"Fine Ale" Destination!

In the *Final Destination* films, there are references to 180, whether it's a flight number, highway number, etc. One thing is for certain. If my friend told me of a premonition of a disaster and my death, I would "180" it and head for the hills!

What film has a premonition about TMZ being mean to Nathan Lane, one last time?
Final "Diss-to-Nathan"!

Oh, Oh, Ohhhhhh! Those were just bewildering! Staggering, even!! I think I'd better watch my step, unlike the escalator victim in *Final Destination 4, The Final Destination!* In fact, I had a premonition that Mr. Bludworth was going to wring my neck for writing these bad jokes!!

Well, I'm going to do that "180" now and head for those hills!! Bye for now!!

This one will knock your socks off! It's a play on a phrase. Ready?
Fly by the seat of my pants!!
See? I told you your socks would pop off! Look! They're hanging

What do you get if you cross legendary jazz vibraphonist, Lionel Hampton, with a Vincent Price character?

The Amazing "Dr. Vibes"

Who do you get crossing the Fantastic Four with the F TROOP show?

The Human STORCH!

What Alfred Hitchcock film "Rocks it Gangnam style"?
PSY-CHO!!

In the film *From Beyond*, Crawford had Christmas trees coming out from his forehead. I guess they tapped into his PINE NEEDLE gland!

What do you get by crossing Louis Armstrong with an underground mutant?

SATCH-MOLE!

CHAPTER 35
CHILDREN OF THE CORN

Children of the Corn was released in 1984. It is directed by Fritz Kiersch and based on a short story by Stephen King about a group of children that follow some type of force in the cornfields. The force tells them through Isaac to kill the town's adult population.

I almost thought I was related to the corn kid followers with my bad jokes and such. But, Isaac put a stop to that! Oh well, I think (yeah, there's something you rarely see. Me thinking!). I think, there's jokes about these cornfield fledglings. Yep! There is!

Here's-12 Bad Jokes About: *Children of the Corn*

What happened to the ancestors of the Children of the Corn when they broke the law?
They were put in the "Stalk-cade"!

Did you know the ancestors of the Children of the Corn were Pilgrims?
Yeah, apparently, they came over on The "Maize- Flower"!

If Chaka Khan is for regular R&B music fans, what musical artist do the Children of the Corn listen to?
"Shucka-Corn"!

What reality game show do the Children of the Corn like?
The "A-Maize-ing" Race!

When playing the game, Clue, what character do the Children of the Corn fight over?
"Kernel" Mustard!

What kids' restaurant do the Children of the Corn go to?
"Shuck" E. Cheese!

What male vocalist do the Children of the Corn like? Chris "Corn-ell"!

What Captain & Tennille song do the Children of the Corn like?
"Husk-rat Love"!

What horror film were the Children of the Corn allowed to watch?
From "Husk" Til' Dawn!

What old time baseball player did the Children of the Corn like?
Ty "Cob"!

What actor did the Children of the Corn hope would raise awareness of corn-based fuel?
"Ethan-ol" Hawke!

What major label wants to sign the Children of the Corn to a contract?
"Green Giant"!

Well, there you have it! Weren't they just awful?! Tell me you don't have a headache by now! Well, what about a laugh or two? Aha! You there! Yes, you! The one reading this in New Hampshire-I heard you laugh! Mission Accomplished!

Remember, Maniacs-There's a bad joke just waiting to be written...

CHAPTER 36
DON'T BE AFRAID OF THE DARK

Don't Be Afraid of the Dark (2010) is directed by Troy Nixey and written by Guillermo Del Toro. It is a remake of a 1973 "made for television" movie of the same name. A girl, a house, and tiny creatures that want your teeth!

Well, why don't we take a look at this film in the way, that only we can! Yes, that's right! Let's chew up 12 Bad Jokes About: *Don't Be Afraid of the Dark!*

"Veni, Vidi, Vici" means "I came, I saw, I conquered." What do the little creatures say to Sally through the air vents?
"Vent-i Vidi Vici" which means: "I talked to you through vents and I'll conquer your teeth!"

What do you get by crossing a Batman film and this remake?
"Don't Be Afraid of the Dark Knight"!

What Stephen King series is about teeth-stealing creatures?
"Don't Be Afraid of the Dark Tower"!

What movie do the little teeth-stealing creatures love?
"TEETH-LESS in Seattle"!

What do you get by crossing Michael Corleone's whimpering brother and this Troy Nixey remake?
"Don't be ALFREDO the Dark!"

The little creatures are planning a television show about tooth removal. It will be called, "THIS OLD MOUTH!"

What Pink Floyd album is dedicated to a film about teeth-stealing creatures?
"Don't Be Afraid of the Dark Side of the Moon!"

What film is about creatures that want to steal "Krispy Kremes?"
"DONUT Be Afraid of the Dark!"

What film about teeth-stealing creatures takes place at a Massachusetts harbor?
"Don't Be Afraid of the DOCK!"

What movie is about creatures stealing the teeth from a UPS guy?
"Don't Be A-FREIGHT of the Dark!"

With the tools that were being used to remove the teeth, you can tell they didn't have a good dental plan!

Teeth-stealing creatures? I'm sorry, but that sounds like a bunch of MOLAR-Key!

Well, there you have it! We told 12 Bad Jokes, by GUM! It's the TOOTH! We had to! It's our duty! Just be careful, if you move into a home where there are voices in the vents. You might get an eavesdropper or creatures wanting your chewy chompers!

CHAPTER 37
THE MONSTERMATT MINUTE

The Monstermatt Minute is the best or worst of the *6Ft Plus Horror Podcast*. This is where I tell my jokes, etc. Strange Jason is the "host with the most" and always introduces me in the funniest of ways! Here are some jokes from the show...

Who is the Minnesota Iceman's favorite musician?
ICE-AC Hayes!

What cold Canadian band do the Nazi Zombies in *Dead Snow* listen to?
CHILLY-Wack!!

What Great White song is featured in *Frozen?*
My, My, My, Frostbitten, Twice Shy!!

In Peter Straub's *Ghost Story*, the Chowder Society was STEWING on a 50-year-old secret. I guess it was no SOUP-rise, that a vengeful ghost wrote them a warning. It even dotted the I's and SPLIT the PEAS!

What film has Dieter Laser surgically connecting drinkers of 20-ounce coffees?
The Human VENTI-pede!!

Uh, oh ... J-Lo wants in on the horror film biz. She's trying to combine a *Friday the 13th* film with one of her snooze fests. Get ready for ... Friday the 13th: Jason Takes the Maid in Manhattan!

What kind of film do you get, by crossing *DEATHBED: The Bed That Eats*, with *The Godfather?*
A film that knows when to "Take it to the mattresses!"

Can the Invisible Man take "selfies?" We'll have to take his word on it. Anyone have his Tumblr link?

There's a game that even had Tony Todd "hooked." Well, his hand anyway; it's CANDYMAN Crush!

"Que Sera, Sera" is to little humans, as "Nosfera, Ferato," is to little vampires. Move over, Robin Thicke! The Wolfman had the true "song of the summer." Yep, it's called FURRED Lines!

What home invasion film is based on Shakespeare's Hamlet?
"Your-ick" Next!

What Swedish horror film is about a vampire poet? Robert Frost-Bitten!

I hear that the vampire in it was "Well acquainted with the night ..."

How are politicians like moisturizing the Hands of Orlac?
They get their palms greased!

In the film *The Shining*, Danny Torrence talks backwards, saying, "Redrum. Redrum. "I'm not amazed. In fact I can talk backwards and you will NOT detect it, in the slightest. Listen: Bob, Level, Radar, Racecar...

What musician wants to be on the soundtrack of a *Toolbox Murders* remake?
M.C. HAMMER!

What film do you get by crossing the Kraft brand with a post-apocalyptic musical?
Six String Cheese Samurai!

Did you know that Snoop Dogg wanted to produce a Twisted Twins film?
He wanted to call it-Dead Hooker's Junk in a Trunk!

The Sharpie company came up with a product for cemeteries. It's called a Grave MARKER!

What movie does the Fly like?
The Great GNATsby!!

What social media do the Killer Tomatoes enjoy?
VINE!!
Mwhuhuahahahaha!

CHAPTER 38
HO HO HORRORDAYS

Well, Maniacs it's "Cryptmas" time! The Monsters and Horror Fiends love this time of year, as do I! In fact, I was running around the crypt, shaking each casket, trying to guess what my gifts are! I couldn't tell!

Mwhuhuhahaha!

Do you want to play "Cryptmas" tree?! Stand in a bucket of water, decorate yourself with lights & plug your fingers into an electrical outlet!!!

Mwhuhuhhahaha!

My Mothra-in-law stuffed my stocking with a candy-cane. It's an Arsenic flavored candy-cane!!

Mwhuhuhahaha!

Dr Jekyll's going "Cryptmas" shopping. He's rather concerned about where to "Hyde" the gifts.

The Wolfman sent me a "Furrier" and Ives card. It says "Happy Howl-idays!"

The Mummy wants to help everyone "wrap" their gifts.

When it comes time for the "Horrordays", The Fly is all abuzz.

At "Cryptmas" time, King Kong doesn't "monkey" around.

Aliens think "Cryptmas" is out of this world!

CHAPTER 39
CRYPTMAS SCARE-OLS

Cryptmas Party

It's that time of year to have good cheer. So come to the crypt for a party!

We'll line the moats with decorated heads that float and have punch with a dash of Bacardi

I'll step out to the porch, to remove the torch, because Frankenstein does not like fire

He'll bring his Bride some fruitcake, made years ago. I don't think those things ever expire!

The Wolfman will lead the Cryptmas Scare-ols, with "Bark, the Hairy Angels Sing"!

He'll put the "harm" in harmonize as the Phantom's fingers tickle the ivories like fluttering vampire bat wings.

We'll exchange gifts. What do you think you'll get?

We got Dracula his very own electric VEIN set.

The cannibals wanted one too,

But only if it had some flesh to CHEW, CHEW.

The Man from the Gallows will hang HORRORnaments on the tree.

The Creature from the Black Lagoon will help too.
He'll get his fins full.

Every year the Cat People can't stop from eating lots of tinsel.

So, we Monsters would love to drop by and call As we wish you, Happy Horrordays, Everyone! One and All!

Hellraiser: Silent Night

Silent Night for the Cenobites.

All is calm in Hell tonight.

Pinhead, Chatterbox, Butterball.

Cringe when someone sings, "Deck the Halls".

They'll tear your soul apart.

Right down to your Hellbound Heart.

Silent Night for the Cenobites.

Will someone open the puzzle box, tonight?

Uncle Frank, Kirsty and Tiffany too.

Dr. Channard or his Julia Boo.

Lament puzzles, times two.

Pinhead has such sights to show you!

Steve Perry's Holiday

'Tis the season to be merry, said Journey singer Steve Perry as he ran to a moving ferry.

His girl waited for him on the deck he shouted: "Hold On, Sherrie"!

The Monster Show
(Tune of "Let It Snow")

Oh, the monsters on film are frightful. And boy, are they delightful!
Let's sit in the front row, of The Monster Show! The Monster Show! The Monster Show!

Let's find some corn for popping.
While monsters are stomping and chomping. Since the blood on film will flow, at The Monster Show! The Monster show! The Monster Show!

When we finally kiss Ghoul night, How I hate going into a swarm,
Of real film monsters with appetites, Our limbs will be ripped and then torn!

The movie house screens are ripping, As the monsters escape, by leaping.
They come to life in throes, at The Monster Show! The Monster Show! The Monster Show!

Quasimodo Sings!!
(to the tune of "I Heard the Bells on Christmas Day")

I rang the bells on Cryptmas Day. In a cathedral known as Notre Dame. I rang bells with my hands and feet. Bell peals on earth, Ghoul will to men.

I sit among my Gargoyle friends. On the roof, our friendship has no end. Their silent stares and grins are sweet, as bell peals on earth, Ghoul Will, to men.

For Esmeralda, my Gypsy Queen, For all of Paris, you remain in my dreams. I gladly make. My. Bells. Ring. For Bell Peals...On Earth... Ghoul Will...To Men!!!!!

A Cryptmas Poem

'Twas the night before Cryptmas, And all through Mattsylvania Vampires ran amuck, you know, the kind that want to drainya?!

They looked for gifts, they looked for blood.
They looked for movies without Jack Black or Paul Rudd.

The Predators set traps by the chimney with care. In hopes that St. Nicholas would soon be ensnared.

The Little Monsters were nestled and snug in their beds,
With visions of Human Centipedes dancing in their heads.

And Mama shrieked!
My face, she did smack!
When I said Twilight made me want to yak!

Then out in the yards, sounds like broken generators.
I jumped to the window, to see the agitators.

A Jersey Shore bunch, completely wasted.
Fist pumping, spray-tan orange and intoxicated.

An ungodly sight, for this hour of night.
I knew what to do, to make things right.

I made calls to the monstrous beings I knew.
Cenobites, Freddy, Jason, Toxie, Michael Myers, Miley Cyrus and Michael Vick to name but a few.
They arrived quickly and gathered a plan.
Mutants, Monsters, Ghouls and Creeps.
Yuck! What a clan!

When, up on the roof, a sleigh did arrive.
With its speakers going "hammer"!
It had such a vibe.

A Demonic elf being, stepped out of the side.

The ghoulish army looked up and wondered, who is this guy?!

He bowed to all, even the fist-pumping crew.
Cracking his knuckles, he said: "Here's what we're going to do."

"I'm the Demon brother of St. Nick, Good Santa Claus.
But, not half as nice as the old 'sugar drawers'.

You've got a problem, no doubt, a total conundrum.
Between those monstrous beings and the spray-tan orangedum-dums.

Someone has to leave, so good folk can get rest.
But before all of that, I want PHAT BEATS!
The ones that are the best!"

And with that he brought out a turntable from his bag.
He spun some PHAT BEATS, no notes that would sag.

The monsters and Jersey dum-dums, started fist-pumping
At first, my hands were in clenches.
The beats were really PHAT, the party got really infectious!

A strange and wonderful party, a horror filled sight.
Zombies, ghouls and mutants on the left. 3D sequels, prequels and remake horrors on the right.

Eventually,
the crowd got sleepy.
Santa Clause's half-brother took a look at the creepies.

He said: "I've got to jet!
It's been real tight!
Merry Cryptmas to All, and to All, a Ghoul Night!!!"

CHAPTER 40
RANCID RHYMES

That's A-Morbid!!
(Tune of "That's Amore")

When a Cannibal guy, takes a bite from your eye,
That's A-Morbid!

When a Killer attacks and he's wearing plaid slacks,
That's A-Morbid!

A Zombie, Vampire too, A Monster for you-It's so scary!
A Warlock, a Ghoul, A Werewolf or two- They're so hairy!

When a Living Dead being crashes onto the scene,
That's A-Morbid!

When the Boogeymen come, they kill just for fun,
That's A-Morbid!

If the marks on your neck, Give way to a credit check, For Nosferatu!
Then, we'll repo his coffin, because payments he's forgotten: To lie there, we forbid!
That's! A-Morbid!

It Came From Outer Space, My Dear

It came from outer space, my dear. In glorious black and white. With 3D elements from the fifties, For a SCI-FI fan's delights. Based on a Ray Bradbury short story, It remains a classic for some. A spaceship crashes into the desert, John Putnam sees and is believed by none!

Close Shave

The Invisible Man had to be brave,
When attempting to clean up, trying to shave.

He had all of the equipment, the tools of the trade.
Just one he lacked, one thing made him rave.
One thing needed for a task with a blade.

A reflection! Was just what he craved.
Without it, a beard he'd grow and save.

Human Centipede Song
(To the tune of "Misty")

Look at me, I'm the first segment of the Human Centipede. They say, three is a crowd. But, it's very clear, my face is up somebody's rear.
Look at me, I have three sets of arms, three sets of knees. Try to learn my lefts, from my rights. I wish I could flee, I'm the Human Centipede.

As the leader of this strange three-pack. I have two more mouths to feed. Because of a scientist quack, there's no chance we'll be freed. All three of us agree...

Look at me, I'm sure we all could use a mint or candy. The problems have only begun. The doctor wants more Human Centipedes.

I'll Be Sealing You
(To the tune of "I'll Be Seeing You")

I'll Be Sealing You, Behind this wall of bricks,
You'll never have wine or chicks, The joke's on you!
You've hurt me, in such a way. That, you won't see the light of day. Jester, Fortunato,
These catacombs Are your final home. I'll Be Sealing You.
The Amontillado, is not here. It never was, Fortunato, dear. Shame on you!
Not even, for "The Love of God" Will I consider freeing you.
You can hope for escape, But, I'll Be Sealing You!

The Living Dead

The resurrected, living dead reek! It's true! They smell like worms, and soil. They look a little chewed. A maggot or two, they might have accrued...

Roosters crow, signaling morn. My jokes clunk, signaling "corn".

The Swedish cousin of PT Barnum, said: "At every moment, a sucker is BJORNE".

Come on down! Come on down! To the strangest show in town! "Torpedoes of Truth" are firing, but the Warlock using them has fried his wiring.

Howling, growling, the fans of JK Rowling. Harry Potter is their wish, the books give a spot of fun. Arriving at the end, they want another one.

After tearing out her eyes out of disgust.
She could bear it no more, she cussed. "TMZ is a garbage pail!" That site gives me the hives! I don't care who's cheating on whom. And who has secret wives.

I'll look for a more informative outlet, too give me straightforward views. Something unbiased, less slanderous, unyielding. Like the straight shooters on Fox News.

Robots, Robots, with their metal shells. Witches, Witches, casting tons of spells. Pauly D. from the Jersey Shore: Applying gobs of hair gel.

Glittering, shimmering, a Vampire series without bite! What could this melancholy snore fest be?! Methinks it is *Twilight*.

To drink, I think, some Tiger Blood, when I could have a "V-8". Is falling prey to trendy things. You do them, but realize-it's not so great!

Goblins eat little kids. They make morsels that are quite tasty. They used to eat burlesque dancers, but choked on the wigs and pasties.

Frankenstein, Frankenstein!
(Tune of Matchmaker, Matchmaker)

Frankenstein, Frankenstein, make me a match. My body parts differ. The one's that you've snatched! With Igor, that crazy, damnable, hunchback-Not one part is like the other!

Frankenstein, Frankenstein, a puzzle am I. With mismatched pieces, that just don't fly! It seems you've given me one person's eye, and one, from somebody's brother!

Seriously! Your needlework's lacking! My stitches, look like railroad tracking! I feel I've taken a shellacking. You take credit, for "creating" life?! Get off, your high horse, you louse! Quickly, make me a spouse! With a bride, I will set up house, and see if our sparks fly!

Frankenstein, Frankenstein, make me a match. Or a plan for your punishment, I will hatch! I'll hold the key to your dungeon latch! You'll, be locked up! If you don't, make me a match! Frankenstein. Make.
Me. A. Match!!!

He hunted, it hid. The silliest thing he ever did. Was try to tame a giant arachnid! When it grew hungry and found him-things hit the skids.

It came to my city, stirred up trouble. Chaos, damage and such. It was The Blob! It ate all it could, then left my hood. Leaving us in Dutch!

My dear, I'm sorry if I snarl. I can't help it. I am a Beast Man. Having hooves for hands is not ideal. If I want to play keyboards in a band...

Putrid Ingrid is a pet Zombie. Tethered to the wall. She's still dangerous, after-all. She might bite you! That's the call!

She trained in martial arts for when the Zombies started attacking. Dead walkers, she'd be smacking! Hear that?! It's skulls she's cracking!

It's a Gamer

Weapons blazing, eyeballs glazing, what is happening that's so darn amazing? It's a gamer and video games he's playing! He needs a bath, it goes without saying.

Hasn't left his apartment in weeks, I'm guessing. So, the place is a sty, he's been messing.
Pizza boxes, take-out containers, it's a strange breed the video gamers.

A Mutant had thoughts of affluence,
But her bankroll and thoughts weren't congruent. It caused anguish, giving her neuroses, that she couldn't ditch, until she was "pushing up posies".

A Golem sat pondering existence and why they invented Sanka. A coffee that's instant. If it's anywhere near the Golem will keep his distance.

Synthetic organisms, we could make. Things with human traits. But, alas, engineers use time, money and brains- Perfecting the "Shakey Weight".

Scales appeared on her face... What was she doing? Plucking her eyebrows or something?!

With scales on her face- No chance to be ready for the gala. For the change was only starting and she didn't want to jilt her fella.

A last-ditch attempt, to transform quickly, led her to sprout scales on her torso. She watched Glenn Beck. His ideology, brought the scales on in bunches, even more so. His show gives people the hives, but her it gives release of the beast within.
Tea Party notions are better than potions, to change a girl into a reptile, with a grin. Change complete- To the gala she went, with her favorite gent, partying until morn

The Beck show gave a gal a chance to change into something, resembling the Gorn.

Lurking, lurking, in the dark ... I wonder where my hearse is parked?!

How many volts, go through the neck-bolts of the one called Frankenstein? He has no count of the exact amount. But, they sure make him feel fine.

Jigsaw's latest trap is an audio one. Music so loud, your ears will bleed. He'll play something to teach ya-Any awful song by Ke$ha.

Sorry, TLC Channel. Your cake baking tyrant on his ear should be tossed. "Father's Day" from *Creepshow* had a better "Cake Boss"!

I'm not sure why they did it. It doesn't make sense. Fast & Furious 5? Someone needed to pay the rent! Please spare us of more "fast" events.

I'm sorry if this turns into a shocker. But, I really don't want to MEET THE FOCKERS. Stiller, Streisand, De Niro, don't give what I'm after. Aren't comedy films made for provoking laughter?!

A bloke, who choked things with his "grippers". Was infamous after being dubbed "Jack the Ripper".

A transaction led to an acquisition of something ancient.

Of this, I'm quite certain. When my assistant trotted in, wearing a stupid grin, asking, "Shall I close the curtains?"

"Not now, let the light in, for I need to begin examining this object we've brought back.
Its label reads that it's a musical cassette tape, with an astonishing 8 complete tracks!"

Godfather's Luca Brasi

Godfather's Luca Brasi Didn't play Yahtzee,
He was a card-playing guy.

He met a cruel death, Could draw no breath From a piano wire necktie.

Jason's Mask

Jason needed a new hockey mask. His had taken a lot of beatings.

He didn't have enough money, though, his was always fleeting.

He looked all over Camp Crystal lake, finding a quarter or two. He called up a financial wizard; TV's own Suze Ormon! She'll know what to do!

She looked over his income, payments and such. Jason was hoping, she'd come through in the clutch!

Suze almost gave him the go-ahead phrase. To make a hockey mask purchase and brighten his days! But, she came upon various travel expenses.

Jason had gone to outer space, Hell, and Manhattan, for instance.

He could not justify his trips to her. She told him "no go", her final word.
He shed a tear, on his disgusting cheek.
Havoc and mayhem, he wanted to wreck.

A wave of sound effects blasted them both! A shouting man said, "Suze Ormon! You're toast!"

He came in a rush, in a blind fury. He said to Jason, "Now buddy, don't you worry. The name's Jim Cramer, MAD MONEY'S my show. I've forgotten more than Suze will ever know. I'll get your mask, if you do me a task. Shut her up for good! Make it last!"

Then, Jason unsheathed his favorite machete. Took a practice swing, so he was good and ready. He struck Suze Ormon square on her head! In fact, it came off; it was a disguise! Underneath, however, was something truly scary: the creator of *Madea*, Tyler Perry! Jim Cramer punched him in the eyes!

Jason gave Jim Cramer his old mask, to retire it on a shelf.

Jim Cramer asked, "What if I wear it and join you in being bad?"

Jason replied: "I'm like Tyler Perry's movie, 'I Can Do Bad All by Myself'!"

Hey Zombo!
(Loosely based on the tune of Hey Mambo!)

A Zombie went to "Dirt Nap-oli" Because, it wanted to feed.
The native flesh, it wanted so. It settled for a big toe!

Hey Zombo! Zombie Italiano! Hey Zombo! Zombie Italiano! Go! Go! Go! You mixed up Walking Dead Paisano! All you Zombies spacey, do the Zombo like a crazy!
Hey Zombo! Don't want any pasta! Hey Zombo! Don't want to eat a Rasta! Hey Zombo! Zombie Italiano! Don't eat a girl named Lana, she's sweating in the sauna!
Hey Ghoul-a, I love when you ramble-a. But take a gamble, learn how to Zombo- If you ain't gonna be a scare, you ain't gonna go nowhere!
Hey Zombo! Zombie Italiano! Hey Zombo! Zombie Italiano!
Go, Go, Joe! Shake like Fulci wants ya! Mangia on the feet, of your Paisano named Pete!
When you Zombo Italianooooo!

Shake-a, Zombie Shake-a, cause you want to eat your maker! Mama say "Stop! Because you can't eat Papa!"
Annndd, Hey, Hey, Ghoul! You don't always have to drool! Make like a graveyard bambino, it's a Zombie scene-o!
Kid, you Living Dead and you got maggots in your head, until you-
Hey Zombo! Zombie Italiano! Hey Zombo! Zombie Italiano!
Ho, Ho, Ho! You rigamortised Paisano!
It's-a forgotten, when you start on the rotting, then you-
Zombo Italianooooooooooo!

That's a nice. UGH!!

Fanged Things

Fanged things, haunt your dreams through. Coming with fury, to tear into you. Some are nasty, it's true! Some are polite, asking- how do you do?

That after the hanging, I'll be in love with you. Oh, after the hanging, I'll still be in love with you.

Monster Body

Inside the body of the Monster, is a palate that no longer functions. That is why it seeks out villagers: It's them he likes munchin'!
He can't stop, at just having one.

After the Hanging
(To the tune of After the Loving)

So, I'll swing you to sleep, after the hanging. With a noose I bought, yesterday. Don't worry about the fit, it'll be your surprise for the day.

It's down to the gallows for some hanging.   It's my favorite part of the day. A favorable breeze gives the bodies some extra sway!

"Thanks for hanging me!" are words I never hear. And, "Thanks for hanging me!" I hope to hear, once in my career!

So, I'll swing to sleep, after the hanging. With a last chance kiss of your lips. Our eyes lock together, before the lever, I flip!

And the crowd gives a cheer, almost -as if they knew!!

THE END

Maniacs! This is a fun HACK-tivity for you to enjoy. You will need a pair of scissors. Some of you may require adult supervision. Some of you may requireadult regular vision. How's your vision?! Anyway, do not cut these out if you're reading the book on Kindle or other digital formats! I'd love to see what combinations you come up with! Use the hashtag: #HaHaHorrorCollectosEdition and show us!

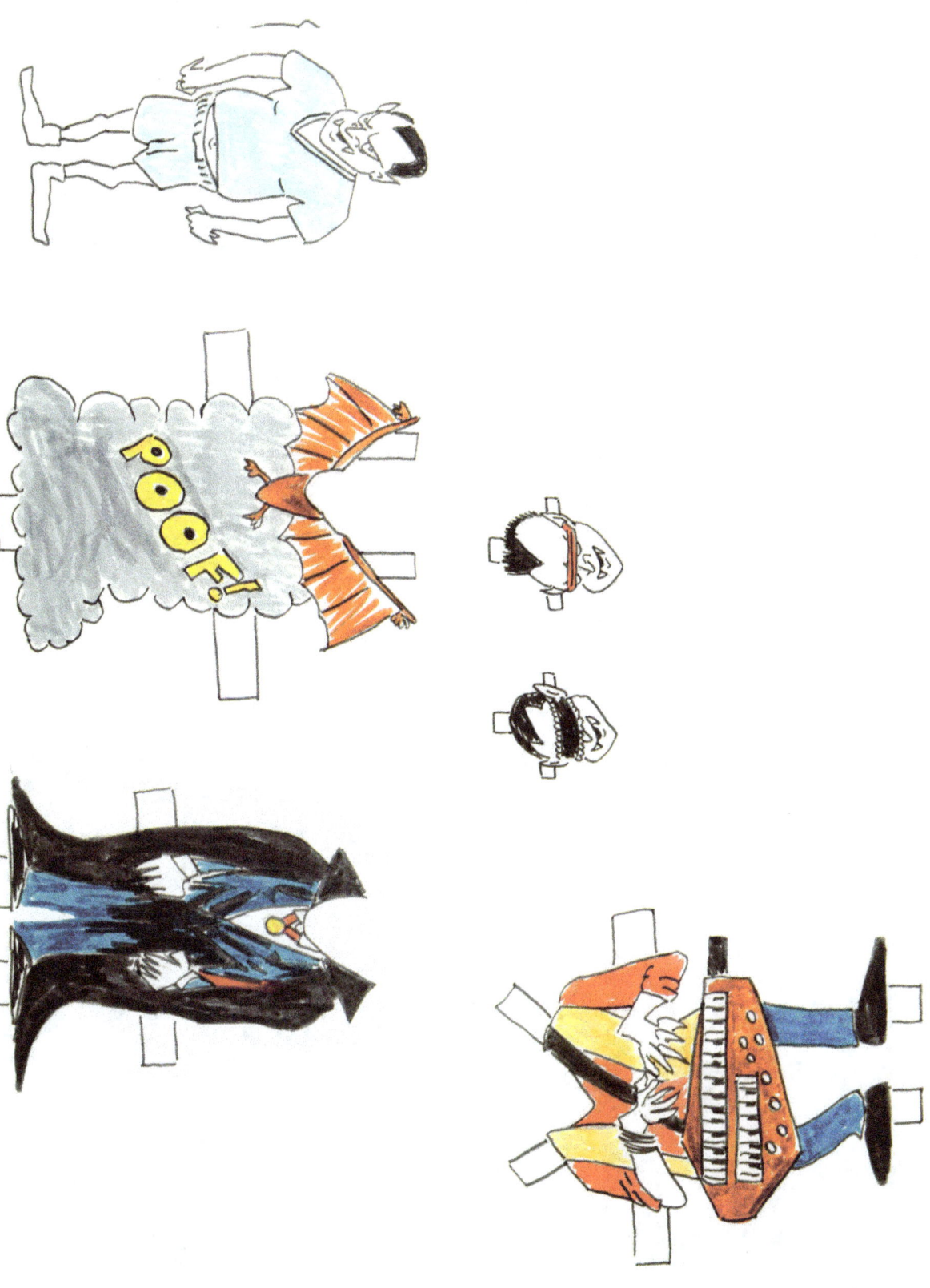

AFTERWORD

By virtue of reading this, you have completed reading Ha-Ha! Horror. You have survived. Congratulations are in order.

Not only have you survived, you have, I assume, finished this book from cover to cover. In doing so, you have irrevocably twisted your mind into something completely unrecognizable by your former self.

The contents within this volume are evidence that Monstermatt Patterson's own brain is undeniably different.
Though his mind is not by any means the most outlandishly deviant mind out there, his jokes are perfect gateways to the bevy of weirdoes, geeks and freaks that exist on the fringes. By reading Ha-Ha! Horror, you've taken that first step to an abnormal life.

Monstermatt's jokes are bad, by design, but they're not horrible and they're not unfunny. Sure, some have set-ups that are more complex than the punchline but you can see Monstermatt's meticulous effort in constructing these jokes. With some, he has reverse engineered a joke, starting with a pun and trying to figure out how it would exist in the world. That is Bad Humor. It's an odd beast, one that invites you to venture beyond the boundaries of convention, to twist reality to conform to you.

What Monstermatt's jokes do best is they hint at a great truth, perhaps the only one there is (or the only one you need.) Monstermatt writes jokes about monsters, monsters we've created to entertain ourselves. Think about it. Fear is felt by all living creatures, a preventive reaction against danger. And yet, we invented mechanisms to stimulate that feeling—namely, horror films and monster movies. We frighten ourselves for entertainment and that, if you don't mind me saying, is bonkers.

Monstermatt takes another primordial reaction—this time, humor—and applies it to these horrible shadows of fearful amusement. We no longer fear, but laugh at that which scares us.

In so, Ha-Ha! Horror has prepared you the key truth about existence. Life, as you will come to know it, is fundamentally absurd.

And that's what you can take away from Ha-Ha! Horror. You'll never be the same from reading this book. How you act now might arouse suspicion by those around you. People might call you mad, demented, or just straight-up weird. All of these are true, of course. But you're one of the initiated, one of the bizarre.

Welcome. It's good to have you here.

Strange Jason
Host of 6FootPlus Horror Podcast

ACKNOWLEDGEMENTS

Monstermatt would like to thank the following people:

Deanna, Sarah, Grant, Emma. My true hearts. With their love and friendship, everything is possible.

My family, from my sisters and step siblings, to my in-laws. From my corny uncles to my cousins.

My father, who again, has told some of the best and worst jokes, ever! The best ones are the ones he did not write! Believe that!

To the first group of roasters/blurbists in my first book. JoeMoe, Rodrigo Gudino, Joe Bob Briggs, Marcy Italiano, LLSoares, Greg Lamberson, Tony Moran, Nick Cato, Cornelius Badmonk and Pat Tantalo.

The current group of fine people, who stepped up to roast, moi: April Burril (Chainsaw Sally), Maria Olsen, Colleen Wanglund, Tomb Dragomir, John Alan Schwartz, Bill Oberst, Jr., Tony Fayville, Assly, Kristian Hanson, Kane Hodder, Michael Aliosi, Dr Gangrene, Chris Alexander, Michael Bonedigger from HorrorNews.Net and Strange Jason. I kept reminding myself, that these people are friends and not to beeaten!

Friends and inspirational beings and institutions that deserve a nod. Without your creations, perspirations, inspirations, helpful hands and interest in the jokes, etc. , it would be pretty boring without the wonderful things you've brought to the world at large!

Uncle Forry-Forrest J Ackerman, Brian Wade, Sybil Danning, Sean Fernald, Melantha Blackthorne, Michael Scirrabassi, Bob Tancelt Bieber, The Gigante Family, Debbie Rochon, Lloyd Kaufman, Frank Henenlotter, Matt Chassin, Jay Mager, Emil Novak, Rod Durick, Colum McKnight, Deftone Pictures Studios, Mike Sciriabassi and family, Adam Steigert, Horror in the Hammer, Terry Kimmel, Michael O'Hear, Ken Cosentino, Monique Dupree, The Witch's Hat podcast, Kelly Said, Twisted Central, Phil Buchanan. Peter Sellers of Sellers &

Newell Books in Toronto, Andrew Robertson, editor of "Group Hex. Vol.1&2", Eric Elliot, editor of Batman Meets Godzilla

Thanks to Julie and Andrew from Cats Like Us, Chris Alexander, Rebekah McKendry, Fallon Masterson and Scars Magazine, Lianne Spiderbaby, Jorge Solis, Shadow Cast Audio, The Horror Writer's Association, Famous Monsters of Filmland, Mad Magazine, Stan Lee, the film, arts and haunted house communities of Western New York, Jesse Zuffle and Club Diablo-RIP Diablo. Monsters For Charity, the #AA's, Jenn & Will Brown, Nora Drogi, McVladie,Tim Hortons, Brian Heiler- Rack Toys-Plaid Stallions- MegoMuseum, Arcana Studios-George Ford- Mike Schneider, Death Shriek, Happy Cloud Pictures, Rick Hipson, The Mommie D Show, Rue Morgue Magazine, TOMBTV!! Shock Horror Magazine, Scream Magazine, Fangoria, Jim Breidenstein, Space Monsters Magazine, The Lair of the Yak, Ray Harryhausen, Jack Pierce, Lon Chaney, Christopher Lee, Boris Karloff, Bela Lugosi, Zacherle, Svenghoulie and all horror hosts, Jimmy O Burril, Troma, HorrorNewsNet, KillerAphrodite.com, GravediggersLocal.com, HorrorSociety.com, Screamwave. Thank you to 6Ft.Plus for using my material and having me on the shows and so many more!

Lon Chaney Sr., the Man of a Thousand Faces - I, the Man of a Thousand Bad Monster Jokes, bow to your masterful expertise, in bringing Quasimodo, the Phantom and many more to the screen. It is my sincerest hope that wherever you are, you accept my humorous homage to your work. The Phantom came to me as the 1000th joke and as the book cover's figure.

I have to thank the North Tonawanda Public Library and its staff for providing so many wonderful books that brought the monstrous and wondrous into my hands for many, many years. It is the cornerstone place that allowed me to revel in that which is scary.

A huge thanks to Clifton Hill-The House of Frankenstein, Dracula's Castle, Shawn Dyck, Mary Ann Robinson and the rest of the people carrying the torches (just not too close to the monsters). It's there and the Maple Leaf Village area that I was shown true terror in the wax figures and monsters that roam the maze-like hallways. To be a part of that rich history is such an honor.

Thank you, Mystery & Horror LLC, Sarah Glenn, and Gwen Mayo. Without your support, effort and belief, this project wouldn't be.

Finally, thank you to every one of the readers and fans. Maniacs, I love hearing your favorite one(s), repeated back to me! Whether you hear me on 6ftplus or enjoy a bit I wrote with Tomb Dragomir, for Tomb TV- I'm glad to keep writing them as long as you're willing to read or listen to them! Speaking of that, I must go write some more Bad Monster Jokes!!!! Igor! Close the laboratory doors. The monster that is Ha-Ha! Horror, must have its Bride. It's time to create!

Maniacs, bye-bye for now. Ouija Board Wishes Cadaver Dreams!

Mwhuhuhuhahahahaha!!!

ABOUT THE AUTHOR

MONSTERMATT PATTERSON

Monstermatt Patterson, The Man of a Thousand Bad Monster Jokes, is a monster of many talents! He started on this journey into horror and monsters, in the Winter of 2006, following shoulder surgery.
His works (Writing or Illustration) are included in:

Rack Toys: Cheap, Crazed Playthings (Painting)
Steampunk Originals Vol.2 (Story and Cartoon)
Death Shriek Comics (Illustration)

Monstermatt's Bad Monster Jokes Vol.1 (Author) -

He regularly appears on 6 FootPlus horror podcast and contributes to Screamwave Podcast, Rotting Flesh Radio, Tomb TV, HorrorSociety.com, HorrorNews.net, TwistedCentral.com, KillerAphrodite.com, Gravediggerslocal.com

Films:(acting, fx, producing, art dept)
Sledge Return to Nuke 'Em High The American Side A Grim Becoming Pigman Dry Bones GoGo Girls vs. the Nazis The Pigman The Night and Final Day To Release a Soul Born to Die Fable: Teeth of Beasts Superheroes Don't Need Capes Beyond the Mainstream   More to come...

Honors

Nominee- 2009 Best Sculptor, Artvoice's Best of Buffalo Awards. 2010 Emcee Buffalo Monster Fest

Nominee- 2013 Best Paintee, Artvoice's Best of Buffalo Awards.

Nominee 2011,2012 6FtPlus - Best Podcast Rondo Hatton Horror Awards

Winner- 2014 Best Painter , Artvoice's Best of Buffalo Awards.

Winner - 2014 President's Choice Gold Medal Award. Florida Publisher's Association Awards.

Nominee- 2014,2015,2016,2017,
6FtPlus- Best Podcast, Rondo Hatton Horror Awards

Nominee - 2016 Book of the Year , Rondo Hatton Horror Awards.